P9-DGQ-127

International and *New York Times* best-selling author

NICK VUJICIC

BE THE HANDS AND FEET

Living Out God's Love for All His Children

WATERBROOK

Be the Hands and Feet

Italics in Scripture quotations reflect the author's added emphasis.

Hardcover ISBN 978-1-60142-620-8
eBook ISBN 978-1-60142-622-2

Cover design by Kristopher K. Orr; cover photography by Mike Villa

Published in the United States by WaterBrook, an imprint of the Crown Publishing Group, a division of Penguin Random House LLC, New York.

Library of Congress Cataloging-in-Publication Data
Names: Vujicic, Nick, author.
Title: Be the hands and feet : living out God's love for all his children / Nick Vujicic.
Description: First Edition. | Colorado Springs : WaterBrook, 2018.
Identifiers: LCCN 2017034906| ISBN 9781601426208 (hardcover) | ISBN 9781601426222 (electronic)
Subjects: LCSH: Witness bearing (Christianity) | Christian life.
Classification: LCC BV4520 .V85 2018 | DDC 248/.5—dc23
LC record available at https://lccn.loc.gov/2017034906

Printed in the United States of America
2018—First Edition

10 9 8 7 6 5 4 3 2 1

I would like to dedicate this book in loving memory of my dad, Boris Vujicic, who went home on May 14, 2017.

I have fought the good fight, I have finished the race, I have kept the faith.

—2 Timothy 4:7

CONTENTS

If God can use a man without arms and
legs to be His hands and feet, then He
will certainly use any willing heart!

—Nick Vujicic

INTRODUCTION

Christ has no body but yours,
No hands, no feet on earth but yours,
Yours are the eyes with which he looks
Compassion on this world.
Yours are the feet with which he walks to do good,
Yours are the hands, with which he blesses all the world.

—Saint Teresa of Avila, "Christ Has No Body"

Your first thought upon picking up this book is probably, *How can a person born without any limbs consider himself to be the hands and feet of Jesus on earth?*

I agree, hands down, that this is a very good question. I asked myself the same thing many times as I was growing up. What purpose could God have for a man with no limbs?

The above quotation from Saint Teresa of Avila had a huge impact on me, as you might imagine. Her words provided one of the many steps I took to finding my purpose as an inspirational speaker and Christian role model who shares his faith with others. I can't do everything, but I do whatever I can to compel people to fill God's house. This is what we are meant to do as Christians, all of us.

The truth of who we are is how we live day to day. If you want to influence others, the most important thing you can do is be a living example of the principles, ideals, and faith that you advocate. This is especially true for Christians. The best way to share your beliefs with others is to live according to your faith when you are under pressure, when challenges arise, and even when life seems to be piling one hardship upon another on you.

Those around you watch and take note of how you respond to life's toughest times. They observe how you love and treat others. They judge your authenticity by how you handle yourself and whether you live up to your claims when the dark days descend.

Part of wisdom is knowing when to react strongly and when to let things pass. It's not about putting up a brave front or a steely smile or being positive just for appearance's sake. It's about drawing strength from deep within and, rather than wallowing in despair, taking one step at a time in positive directions.

I've written and spoken often of the challenges I've faced in life because I was shorted the standard allotment of limbs at birth. In describing my journey, I've noted my early crisis of faith, my despair and depression that led to an attempted suicide, and how I eventually came to understand that I was not God's mistake but instead that God did have a plan and a purpose for His "perfectly imperfect child."

My life story has been well chronicled in my earlier books, in my father's book about raising me, and in my many speeches and videos. This book covers some recent major events—and a few scares—in my life, but it is more about my *life's work,* how I found my calling as the hands and feet of Jesus on earth, how a few recent challenges have affirmed and strengthened that calling, and how I think you and I can expand our influence and bring more of God's children to Him by living our faith and inspiring, loving, and serving others.

I thought about calling this book *Adventures in Evangelism,* but unfortunately, the term *evangelism* has been tarnished with negative connotations over the years in some areas of the world. I get it.

Too many people have been put off by overzealous Christians who probably had good intentions but reached out with poorly conceived strategies. They may have come across as pushy or more concerned about their agendas than the feelings and beliefs of those they approached.

I believe all Christians have a responsibility to share their faith and bring others to Christ. His followers are, after all, "fishers" of men and women. We can't just be passengers in the boat. We need to cast our lines, because there is an ocean of people out there who need the redemptive power of God's love. My hope is that this book will inspire you to find your own way to do that in a manner that best suits you and best serves our heavenly Father.

There are many praying for *revival,* another word actually that has been overused, particularly in the US and other western parts of the globe. What does that revival even look like? I personally just want to fulfill the mandate to preach the gospel and see people come to Jesus, start an active relationship with Him, be transformed by that daily, and become true followers of Him.

Many await a movement, when actually the basic thing God has asked of us—to tell others that He lives—doesn't always happen. We say, "God move." God says, "I will move through you when you move."

Part I

Letting your Light Shine

1

CALLED TO SERVE

I certainly didn't start out thinking I would be God's hands and feet, an evangelist proclaiming the good news. In fact, even though I grew up in a strong Christian family with a father who was a lay pastor, I confess I was among those teenagers who shunned "the God squad" in school for a time. I wanted to be cool, and talking about your faith to other teens wasn't considered cool at all.

I had to get comfortable with myself and my beliefs before I could ever be comfortable and effective in sharing my faith with other people. Even after I accepted Jesus Christ as my Lord and Savior, I wasn't inclined to go forth and save the rest of the world at first. I wanted to be a professional soccer player, but I am built so low to the ground, league officials ruled no one would be able to stop me. So I had to pursue a different career, just to keep it fair for the other blokes.

Once playing for Manchester United was ruled out, I wasn't sure what to do with myself. My dad, the lay pastor, thought I'd be much better off as an accountant, and for lack of other options, I went along with that.

I never considered that my faith would become a career because it was such a personal and intimate aspect of my life. Our family church was the Apostolic Christian Church of the Nazarene in Keilor Downs in the state of Victoria. My memories of going there are mostly focused on being with my parents and my brother and sister and all my aunts, uncles, and cousins. Worship was a very social experience for me.

My father sang tenor and my uncle Ivan sang bass in the church choir. As founding pastors of the congregation, they'd sit in the front row with the other choir members. I joined them as the unofficial percussionist. I kept the beat by tapping my little foot on a hymnal book, which substituted for a drum. Later they bought me a drum machine and eventually a keyboard I could play with my foot. I loved music and it was one of my favorite parts of church. I associated God with everything I loved.

My father always talked about God on a very personal level, and I picked up on that. I conversed with God all the time, it seemed. He was very real to me, like a member of the family or a good friend. I felt like He knew everything about me and I could talk to Him about everything. He was real to me and always there for me. God wasn't a father figure or a vengeful power; He was more like an older, wiser mentor and friend.

I prayed every night, but I didn't think of myself as religious. I didn't dream of being a pastor. Our family just lived in faith. To me, being Christian was like being Serbian or Australian. I didn't think there was anything special about it, and I certainly didn't feel I was holier than anyone else.

I felt guilty for years because I had unholy thoughts when our family friends, Victor and Elsie Schlatter, gave a slideshow presentation on their missionary work in the wilds of New Guinea. They had translated the Bible into pidgin English for the natives there, and they recruited hundreds of them to Christianity. It was hard to believe that there were people who had never heard about Jesus Christ. I assumed He was known about by all.

I confess, though, that what left the biggest impression on me from their slideshow were the photos of naked New Guinea women. That probably wasn't what they'd hoped I'd remember about their presentation, but, hey, I was just a boy being a boy. I was easily distracted. Especially by Miss Isabell, our Sunday school teacher. She had short blonde hair, big blue eyes, and an engaging smile. I thought she was really pretty. I had a crush on her!

I was no saint, believe me. I got in trouble more than a few times for chewing gum in church, and one Sunday I choked on a piece of candy just before the service started. Since we were seated in front, the entire congregation saw my dad grab me, turn me upside down, and slap me on the back to dislodge the candy.

SEARCHING FOR ANSWERS

That would not be the last time I was saved in church. Other kids could release their nervous energy during services by tapping their feet on the kneelers or drumming their fingers on the pews. When I was antsy, I'd go to the very last pew in the back of the church and rub the back of my head on the brick wall. Crazy, I know! Thanks to that bad habit, for a while I was the youngest person in our church to have a bald spot.

I was a little goofy as well as easily confused. I was totally baffled when a South American immigrant named Jesus showed up in our first-grade elementary school class.

"Why do they call you Jesus?" I asked, wondering if we were at the end of times when Jesus was to return as the Messiah.

I was very suspicious because our Sunday school class had taught us that when the devil showed up, he'd claim to be Christ. I was on the lookout for imposters. Poor Jesus, my classmate, didn't understand why I kept interrogating him about his name.

I took my Sunday school teachings seriously. When I was six or seven, after we learned about the second coming of Jesus Christ, I had a dream about the rapture. In my dream, I was visiting my grandparents' house just around the corner from the church, and I saw all these angels come down and take people up. I saw one of my family members go up, and I waited, but no angel came for me. I desperately, and sadly, thought, *Where is my angel?* Then I woke up, which was a relief!

I didn't want to be left behind, so I doubled down on trying to be a good Christian boy. Every Sunday in church, the pastor would ask if we had Jesus in our hearts, and I always answered yes as loudly as I could in case the angels were listening. We were taught that to be Christians we needed God in our lives every day. I wasn't afraid to tell people that I went to church, but we weren't taught to talk about Jesus with our friends who weren't Christians. We were supposed to keep it to ourselves and love everyone. I don't remember ever praying openly for friends to accept Him into their lives. Instead, I did it privately so they never knew what hit them!

The only evangelists we talked about were heroic missionaries like the Schlatters, our family friends. Victor and Elsie became mentors to me later in life. They were the first true global soldiers of Christ I ever knew. Victor was like a Bible character, a big man with long gray hair and a gray beard bigger than my head. They made missionary work sound so exciting. They told us cool stories about life in the rain forest and being chased by people who didn't like Christians.

I was in awe of them. They were so exotic, like Indiana Jones meets Billy Graham. In their younger days, my parents had considered working in New Guinea as missionaries with Victor and Elsie. On their honeymoon, they even visited the Schlatters to check it out, but my dad said it was too wild for him. I often imagined what my life would have been like if they'd decided to stay in New Guinea. I am thankful my family stayed in Melbourne.

A GREATER VISION

> Therefore, we are ambassadors for Christ, God making his appeal through us. (2 Corinthians 5:20)

Truthfully, I didn't think I would ever be a missionary, because the Schlatters were special people who managed to live and thrive under extremely tough conditions. Still, they inspired me to do whatever I could to help the poor around the world.

They projected their slideshows on the wall at our church, and you'd see all these naked children eating what looked like roots and bugs. We prayed for them and raided our piggy banks to help feed and clothe them. I really admired Victor and Elsie for dedicating their lives to serve as God's ambassadors.

I was in my early teens when I heard a very dramatic story of a missionary whose plane crashed in a remote area of Papua New Guinea. He was taken prisoner but escaped. I saw an interview in which he said it would have been impossible for him to get out of there, but God made all his captors deaf so he could free himself, take possession of their plane, and get away. The film is called *Ee-Taow*.

Then I read *The Heavenly Man* by the Chinese evangelist Brother Yun, a leader of the underground Christian church movement there. I could relate to Brother Yun's stories of being imprisoned and tortured by government authorities in China; my parents and grandparents had fled Serbia because of the persecution of Christians there.

Yun's book said that God always stepped in to protect him at the worst times. During his stay in prison, Brother Yun escaped death on many occasions. He was supposed to be hanged, but whenever his time came, the executioner claimed to be too tired or somehow paralyzed. The executioner eventually told Yun that he would make sure he was not killed inside the prison.

Brother Yun also writes of escaping from a maximum-security prison by listening to the voice of the Holy Spirit when it told him to just walk out the prison gate one day. He followed those instructions and walked out without being challenged by the guards; it was as if he were invisible. Though many have argued that his story does not sound plausible, the Chinese government said his escape was "an embarrassing mishap."

I was in my teens when I read Brother Yun's book and the books of another brave Christian role model, former New York City gang leader Nicky Cruz. His *Run Baby Run* is a classic story of a troubled street kid who turned his life around through Christ and became a missionary to other young people.

The inspiring 1970 movie about his life, *The Cross and the Switchblade,* has been viewed by more than fifty million people in 150 countries. Like Brother Yun, Nicky Cruz endured many hardships, but God seemed to step in whenever his life was threatened. He writes of having a gun pointed at his head, but when his would-be killer pulled the trigger, the gun misfired, saving his life.

Books like *The Heavenly Man* and *Run Baby Run,* along with the stories told by the Schlatters, later gave me the courage to leave the security of my family and home at the age of nineteen and make my first trip as a Christian speaker to South Africa. They taught me there is no safer place to be than where God leads you.

When we are young, most of us can't see or even comprehend what God has planned for our lives. Yet looking back now, as I enter my midthirties after already traveling millions of miles and speaking to millions of people, I can see the influences and experiences that led me to His path.

I have to laugh, especially when I think how puzzled I was as a boy when my Uncle Sam patted my head and said, "One day, Nicky, you will be shaking hands with presidents."

I certainly could not see that happening at the time. God must have been whispering into my uncle's ear, because I've met more than a dozen presidents and heads of state over the years. Now I've yet to shake hands with any of them, for obvious reasons, but I've hugged most of them!

ENCOURAGERS AND GUIDES

As I've written before, my other influences as a teenager included my high school's janitor, Mr. Arnold. For some reason, everyone called him Mr. Arnold even though Arnold was his first name. I never knew his last name, but he was always there for me and the other students. He encouraged me to talk openly about my struggles with my disabilities and my faith, first with the students in the Christian teen group he led and then with other students and groups around the area.

I didn't think of myself as an evangelist even remotely at that point. I was more interested in breaking down barriers between people and simply sharing how I did not think hope existed until I allowed God to help. Over time, I saw that my stories inspired others, especially when I explained how I finally came to understand I wasn't one of God's rare mistakes and that we are all beautiful and perfect creations in His eyes.

When I heard my first professional motivational speaker, Reggie Dabs, who gave a talk at my high school, he quieted nearly fourteen hundred restless students and left them inspired simply by telling his life story, which was a message of hope: "You can't change your past, but you can change your future."

Reggie showed me there could be a path to a career in public speaking. Because of the times in my life when I felt different due to my lack of limbs, I always made it a point in my speeches to tell everyone they were beautiful and loved by God. I thought it was something people should hear. We are all beautiful as God's creations.

Even when I began to see myself growing into a career as a professional speaker, my focus was more in the inspirational and motivational realm. I knew many people did not want to hear a faith-based message, but as they heard me talk about life, love, hope, and faith in general terms, they felt free to ask questions about faith. Even then, I still didn't see myself as a role model for other Christians or aspiring Christians.

My dad didn't either. He kept encouraging me to get degrees in accounting and business. I took his advice, figuring it wouldn't hurt to have a backup plan if speaking didn't work out.

FINDING A PATH

Again, God stepped in very quietly and gave me a little nudge back in the direction of His chosen path for me. I was asked to be a volunteer religious education teacher at my old high school in my spare time. They had recent grads come in to give four lessons a week, talking about God and the Bible.

I found myself in front of teen audiences at my old school, sharing my faith and encouraging others in their beliefs. I didn't think of this volunteer job as recruiting believers to Christ, but in retrospect, it was good training for that. I have never written about this because it's a bit of a touchy subject, since around this time there was a little backlash within my own church because I'd been invited to speak at other churches in the area.

At the time, my family church was very insular. They didn't like members of the congregation visiting other churches, probably because they feared losing them. Even my parents and some relatives told me I shouldn't speak at any other churches.

I understood where they were coming from, but I thought all Christians should embrace each other, put aside their doctrinal differences, and focus on our shared love of God. My mission was to share my testimony to encourage all to trust in God. A friend, Jamie Pentsa, encouraged me to accept invitations from all over the area, and he volunteered to drive me to them in his Volvo.

I spoke mostly to other youth groups at first, offering lessons from

Scripture that had impacted me. Those presentations became so popular I put together a monthly newsletter that I delivered to people on an e-mail list. I also developed my own website so people could access my writings and contact me if they wanted me to speak somewhere.

Soon I was receiving more than seventy invitations a week to speak to Bible clubs, youth groups, and church congregations throughout the region. That response inspired me to record my testimony in churches with a video crew. I sent those first *Life Without Limbs* DVDs out to anyone who requested them on my website.

One or more of those videos reached South Africa, where a man named John Pingo saw it. He contacted me and offered to set up a speaking tour around that country. That trip, which my parents had many reservations about, marked the beginning of my international outreach, which to this day has taken me to more than sixty countries around the world. As opportunities came, God also moved other friends, cousins, uncles, and even my brother to take me places, serve as caregivers, and help me encourage more people—and even see some saved.

A GOD-GIVEN EVOLUTION

My career as a Christian role model and inspirational speaker was an unexpected blessing, and looking back, surely part of God's plan for me. My passion for it grew with each engagement. Coming from a childhood when, at times, I felt there was no hope for my future, I was exhilarated by the enthusiastic responses to my speeches and videos. For a man who once had no hope, there can be nothing more rewarding than giving hope to others. The fact that as a young guy I could share my feelings about the gospel of Jesus with large groups of people of all ages gave me a sense of purpose. I felt I could make a contribution, which was so important to me. And I felt closer to God, because so many came forward at altar calls and gave their lives to Christ.

I also witnessed the power of the gospel. To me, 80 percent of inspiration is telling stories. So much of what is in the Bible is encouragement found in stories and testimonies, stories that inspire faith, stories of God's faithfulness. As you read the Word, it produces faith.

I've rarely shared this, but when I was about twelve years old, I was coming out of a dark period of depression. I had this strong compulsion to learn as much about God as I could, so I starting typing out the entire Bible on my computer, using my little foot to peck away.

I started with Genesis 1, the beginning. I was about halfway through Genesis when my mum came into my room, heard me pounding away at the keyboard, and asked what I was doing.

"I'm writing out the Bible," I said.

"Nicky," she said, "it's already written."

She had a point. I could only type about eighteen words a minute back then. I eventually realized I'd taken on a much bigger task than I could complete. My compulsion ended, but my love for God's Word has never diminished. Every time I read the Bible, I learn something new, something deeper and more meaningful. My reverence for God and my personal love for Jesus grow with each fresh viewing.

SHARING FAITH

A big part of being a Christian is sharing what God means to you in a way that is relevant to others. That is how faith comes alive. When I began sharing my testimony to more and more people, the general thinking among Protestants, in my young eyes, was that to bring more people into their churches, all they had to do was tell strangers they loved them and be generous.

This was supposed to convince others that Christ followers were good and kind. The idea was to plant seeds of faith in them through example so they would be drawn to Christians and want to know more. The problem with that is there are other good and kind people in the world, including many Hindus and Muslims.

Followers of Jesus need to be more than good and kind. We need to have powerful messages to share. When I told my dad that I was writing this book he said, "People think it's complicated, but it's not complicated to evangelize at all. We should be ready to share our faith at any time, and it comes down to sitting someone down face to face and just being real. Tell them *what* Jesus means to you. Tell them *how* your life changed after meeting Jesus. Being a believer will show also with how one lives."

The Bible says, "You will recognize them by their fruits." Inspiring others to become good Christians requires reaching out and motivating people to think about the importance of God in their lives, but you have to be prayerfully wise about your communication. You have to adjust your approach to each individual because we all have different personalities and experiences. First Peter 3:15 says, "But in your hearts set apart Christ as Lord. Always be prepared to give an answer to everyone who asks you to give the reason for the hope that you have. But do this with gentleness and respect" (NIV).

"WALKING AROUND" CHRISTIANITY

My natural progression into serving as the arms and legs of Jesus included some early "walking around" Christianity—with a dog. Starting when I was seventeen years old, I would go out in my wheelchair to take our dog for a walk and strike up conversations with almost everyone I met.

I don't know whether it was the cuteness of our dog, Seth (a Jack Russell terrier and Cavalier King Charles spaniel mix), or just me, but there always seemed to be plenty of folks who'd talk or converse while walking alongside us.

We'd talk about the dog, and if we'd never met, they'd often get around to asking how I'd lost my limbs. When I shared my story, they'd be intrigued or touched. These conversations sometimes led to discussions of faith. They wondered sometimes how I could have such a positive attitude, and I'd tell them I believed God created me for a purpose and I'd put my faith in that.

I would offer to pray with those who seemed interested. I don't know whether they were moved by my faith or something else, but it wasn't unusual for people to shed a tear or two when I talked to them about the importance of God in my life and being thankful for the blessings He gives.

Walking around, sharing my dog, Seth, and my faith, became a real passion for me. I'd leave the house with Seth and couldn't wait to see who would come around the corner. After a while, I'd offer to share my story and my beliefs just about anywhere I went. I don't remember being rejected by anyone, though there were probably some who took a detour when they saw me coming.

I tried not to be hard core or high pressure. I would just ask how they were doing, and after a few minutes of conversation, I might say, "Is there anything you'd like me to pray for on your behalf?" Most people appreciated the offer. Who doesn't need a prayer now and then either for themselves or someone they care about? It's like being offered a surprise gift by a stranger, and it's even better than winning the lottery because the prize of prayer is everlasting!

ALTAR CALL

My first big speaking event was at the Logan Uniting Church in Springwood, Queensland. Youth pastor Jim Haak, who was a high school chaplain in the area, heard me speak at an event and then invited me to attend their Year 10 Conference, along with about three hundred high school sophomores. He didn't ask me to be a speaker, just to attend, so I brought along some friends and cousins.

The tenth year of school in Australia is when many teens decide whether to continue their schooling or look for a job. This conference was designed to help them develop some life skills that would be useful either in college or in the working world. Faith was a big part of it, but there were outdoor activities, forums, workshops, and inspirational and motivational events.

Be the Hands and Feet

The Day Nick Became an Evangelist . . . and Joined a Motorcycle Gang

By Jim Haak

That morning I heard a lot of commotion and a ruckus somewhere. The crowd included a whole bunch of boys and some were from rough backgrounds. I thought it was a fight. I went to break it up, but when I walked through the crowd, I realized they were all gathered around Nick!

They were captivated by this young guy with no arms and legs who was playing his unique version of handball with some other kids. He was bouncing the ball off his head and kicking it in the air with his little foot. He was very skillful and everyone wanted to have a look.

Of course, he was also speaking quite loudly and using all the Australian colloquial language. He was solid in his faith but not pious or overly religious. He knew how to draw in a crowd even then.

Nick turned out to be an attraction just by himself that day. Kids gathered around him everywhere he went. The counselors all marveled at the way girls and boys alike were drawn to him, telling him their fears and troubles, bowing their heads as he prayed for them. He was so open and vulnerable that they felt safe confiding in him. They knew just by looking at him that Nick had overcome suffering and bullying too. They trusted him and believed him when he told them, "I love you."

The final event that day was the keynote message and a forum on the main stage. It had been a long, hot day. This God Squad fellow was supposed to give a presentation, but he couldn't get his PowerPoint program to work. The natives were getting restless. He looked at me and said, "I'm having trouble here. Can you entertain the crowd for a while?"

I was sitting on stage with a panel of experienced youth workers, so I turned to them and said, "Does anybody have a joke they can tell?"

Just then Nick came forward and said, "I'll talk to them!"

"What are you going to say, Nick?" I asked.

"Don't worry. I'll just talk to them," he said.

I was still thinking the God Squad guy would get his act together, but I gave Nick the okay to talk just a bit. First, though, we had to figure out how to get a microphone on him since he couldn't hold it. We fussed around and finally Nick said, "Don't worry. I've got this."

The natives were even more restless at that point, and we needed to fill the dead time for our final speaker. I was a little worried about putting poor Nick out there in front of them all. I shouldn't have worried.

After a few words, the entire audience was silent. Nick captivated them all just by talking about the challenges he'd faced being without limbs and so different from everyone else. He talked about his faith as a source of strength, and he told them that God's love could sustain them all, but he didn't push his beliefs on them.

In many ways, it was a standard motivational speech, yet Nick tells his stories with so much passion, humor, and power that the message seems fresh and more engaging. When he encourages people, telling them they can do anything they want to do if they believe in themselves, Nick brings a deeper meaning to the message. Young people who were struggling knew he understood them. Kids who felt like outcasts knew he had faced shunning and bullying too. The toughest kids admired his courage and candor. Everyone wanted to be Nick's friend, and he encouraged them all to treat each other with respect.

We learned that Nick isn't about simply entertaining people. He deals with really hard issues, very real things, not only faith, but about the challenges of life. He talks about realizing that while his disability is a burden, it could also be a gift, which is a message from the gospel itself: "Blessed are the poor in spirit." Nick is humble, but he has the kingdom and he is happy to share it. God uses the ordinary and the simple, the broken and the wounded. He uses them to transform and redeem.

Honestly, we were all awestruck that day. Even the God Squad biker fellow who was supposed to be the main speaker surrendered. His PowerPoint presentation was ready, but he didn't want to follow Nick on that stage.

"Don't worry. He got it just fine," he whispered to me as Nick was wrapping up.

Even though Nick had done a tremendous job just stepping in, I was more than a little skeptical when he extended an invitation at the end of his speech, saying that if anyone needed a bit of love, they could come up and give him a hug.

The other forum leaders and I quietly scoffed, thinking there is no way any of these teenagers would want to be caught dead hugging someone in public. They may be more open to that in the United States, but Australia has a much more reserved and hardnosed culture. Aussies don't show their softer emotions—or so we thought.

Nick made fools of us for doubting his power to reach an audience. Kids came pouring out of their chairs and quietly formed a long line in front of Nick, which was a miracle in itself. Many of them had tears in their eyes after embracing him. Our entire panel of veteran youth workers watched with our jaws dropped. We had never seen anything like this!

After the last hugger had moved on, I went down to talk to Nick. He was so gifted, I figured I'd book him for the next year's forum. Just as I was walking down, Nick headed toward the parking lot in his wheelchair, surrounded by his new fans.

Before I could catch up to him outside, one of the God Squad motorcycle club members came roaring up on his Harley-Davidson. Another biker lifted Nick onto the back of the motorcycle, and they zoomed off with Nick screaming, "Woo-hoo!"

And that was our introduction to the soon-to-be famous Nick Vujicic!

It was a crazy, fun event. There was even a booth manned by members of a Christian motorcycle gang called The God Squad. They were some scary looking, leather-wearing soldiers of Christ with really loud bikes who considered themselves counterculture faithful.

When you get that many Aussie teenagers in one place, things tend to get rowdy, so when Pastor Haak noticed a big crowd gathered in one area and heard some people shouting, he thought a fight had broken out. In fact, I had become something of a curiosity, but Jim tells the story better than I do in the sidebar on the previous pages.

FINDING AN AUDIENCE

I have to say that day at the Year 10 Conference had a huge impact on me as well. Everything just fell into place so naturally, and the teens and the motorcycle guys and the counselors were all so receptive and welcoming. I was just overwhelmed. The capper during my talk was when I saw a girl crying as she raised her hand to get my attention.

She asked if she could come up and give me a hug. I said, "Sure, please do." When she got to me, she gave me this huge, wraparound hug and whispered in my ear, "No one has ever told me that they loved me. No one has ever told me that I am beautiful the way I am."

Whoa! That was when I knew I was born to be a speaker who communicates messages of hope. Later that year, Jim asked me to speak at his church youth group. Many people wept as I shared the truth of how Jesus changed my life. I invited the crowd to silently say a prayer to Jesus right there and then.

After the presentation, I hugged and talked with many people. One girl came up and said, "I've just given my life to Jesus tonight, and I know I will never be the same again." My world stopped right there—it seemed to go from black and white to color.

This was the first time someone shared directly with me that I'd helped them accept Jesus as their Savior, and I was blown away. Having that effect on someone was intoxicating for me. It was like the smell of apple blossoms, and I wanted more and more of it. I knew it was not me or my words. God was working through me.

Another blessing from that day was that Jim Haak became a mentor to me. At the time, I still had some doubts that I could make a living as a public speaker, let alone as a Christian role model. I told him my goal was to be a successful businessman and make a lot of money so I could support myself, because I didn't want to be a burden on my family for the rest of my life.

Jim quietly said he thought I could be an even better professional speaker. He was very kind to me. I think he was the first to tell me that the obstacles in my life could serve as stepping-stones rather than barricades.

Jim and the other youth counselors at that event began inviting me to speak at every event in the area. They were among those who coached me with speaking tips and helped me to refine my message.

My vision for my life was still a little hazy at that point, but it was coming into focus quickly. It was at an event during this time, probably one put on by Jim Haak, that I was introduced to a youth group as evangelist Nick Vujicic for the first time. I hadn't requested that introduction, and at first it threw me off.

Evangelist? Me?

And then I felt this passion well up in my heart to let the world know that Jesus wants to live in us all.

My next thought was quite simply, *Why not give it a shot?*

God opened the door, and His child with no arms and no legs walked through it.

2

ANSWERING QUESTIONS

I work both sides of the fence in my dual speaking careers. Many have heard me speak about spiritual matters in churches, where I also make altar calls in my mission to bring as many people to God as I can. Yet even more people around the world know me as an inspirational speaker to secular audiences in schools, national education systems, corporations, business leadership conferences, and government agencies.

Our mission at Life Without Limbs is to reach the whole world with the gospel and encourage all people in their walk as disciples of Jesus. A 2017 United Nations report says that by 2030 there will be more than 8 billion people on earth, and so I bought Internet domains referring to 8 billion souls to use one day for our ministry.* I created a clear strategy in 2002 and wrote it down in my journal. I cannot just be on faith-based platforms to reach everyone. I will have to go in the marketplace,

* United Nations Department of Economic and Social Affairs / Population Division, *World Population Prospects: The 2017 Revision, Key Findings and Advance Tables,* New York, 2017, https://esa.un.org/unpd/wpp/Publications/Files/WPP2017_KeyFindings.pdf.

government platforms, and education systems where I may not be able to preach but where I still can plant seeds of love and hope.

My Christian beliefs are made clear in those secular speeches, in a personal manner because my story would not be told in full without mentioning my spiritual journey. Most of the time, the clients who are paying me to speak ask that I keep my spiritual content to a minimum or to nothing at all. Sometimes the executive team organizing a conference will ask me for reassurance before the event to make sure I keep my talk secular, while a few in the group may quietly ask me to share more.

God generously gives wisdom and discernment each time. I try to be respectful, and God leads me on stage, helping me know how much to say, if anything, that touches on faith. I've been known to push the envelope even when my sponsoring governments are against religious expression. I cautiously take each opportunity to say just a little so I can return to say more another day. This allows me to have more of a long-term impact in each country.

The reason I do not just talk on platforms that are faith-based is because I want to reach people where they are in the world. You can't save the lost by looking for them inside churches. They are out in the world. When people ask why I accept invitations into countries that restrict or forbid Christians, I tell them I must go where people need to learn about God. That is my underlying strategy.

I consider every appearance to be an opportunity to share my faith, either quietly or overtly. People often approach me with questions about faith. Whether it's on airplanes, in airports, in shops and restaurants, or on the street, I get many requests to pray with strangers.

Many will stop me to share their doubts, misgivings, or heartfelt questions. I've had people tell me they gave up on God after something terrible happened to them or a loved one. They want to know how I can have so much love for a God who brought me into this world without the standard limbs package.

Some are more artful in their queries than others: "Nick, why aren't you angry at God? I mean, He screwed you after all!"

After so many years I can handle most questions like those and others on faith, but I certainly understand why many Christians find it challenging to share their beliefs in spur-of-the-moment situations.

On a trip to China in 2016, a man approached me and asked questions during a fund-raising auction and banquet. His timing wasn't great since the auction was under way, and anybody who talked could have been mistaken for a bidder.

After introducing himself, he asked for advice on being a good parent. I didn't want to get into a discussion out of fear the auctioneer would think I was trying to buy one of the high-priced items up for bid. All I could think to say to the man, in a subdued voice, was, "Love God and pray a lot."

He chuckled at that and said, "My wife is Christian. She prays. I'm not a Christian. I don't believe in God. We've had discussions on whether our kids should go to church or not."

He was sincerely looking for answers, and even though it wasn't the best situation for a serious discussion, I didn't want to brush him off. I believe all Christians have a responsibility to share their faith, especially when a nonbeliever politely asks questions. So he and I went to a quiet place to talk. I shared the abbreviated version of my journey of faith. Then he asked typical questions for a nonbeliever, and I offered my responses.

Our discussion was candid and cordial. We were trying to understand each other's point of view rather than staging a debate. I had a couple of advantages. I've had many, many such conversations, and of course, I like to remind myself, too, that I have God on my side! He knows exactly what needs to be said and how to say it, and He will move through me as I step out in faith-filled action.

As our conversation came to an end, he thanked me with tears in his eyes and said his life would never be the same. I asked if I could pray for him and he consented. I don't know for certain if he became a believer or if he later gave his life to God, but my impression was that God used me to put him on that path. If so, I am grateful for that opportunity to share my faith, as well as all the other opportunities I've had and hope to have.

For these opportunities you have to be prepared and knowledgeable on some levels of course. Sometimes nonbelievers are experienced at debating, and they may be determined to convince a believer that Jesus is not real. They may want to test whether you are really convicted by your beliefs and knowledgeable about the Bible. At the same time, don't be fooled into thinking that God cannot use you even if you feel you lack understanding of all aspects in the faith.

It's not about seeing America becoming a Christian country. It's about fulfilling our Father's desire that all may know Him. When we first find Jesus in our lives, we get fired-up to tell everyone. That fire sometimes fades a bit if we feel the need to be perfect and all-knowing of Scripture before we can share. Some may feel unprepared unless they go to a Bible school or seminary. I've had people say at first they feel naked and exposed when asked questions.

Christians have to be on their toes and ready to share their faith, but many do not know where to start. Fortunately, I actually have a couple of toes, so that's not a problem! The greatest way to demonstrate our faith is to live each day with strength, peace, love, and joy—even amid trial.

But what do we do when God prompts us to share our faith with nonbelievers?

I love my cousin, Daniel, not only because he is my cousin but also because he makes me a better Christian. He comes across strong at times, and he is passionate when he talks about helping the poor. Daniel is not a believer in the idea that Jesus is Lord, and Lord above all.

Even though our extended families were raised in church, several individuals do not believe in the Bible's teachings. There are times when children are force-fed "church," and they may question the teachings, especially when they see church leaders disagree and members cause disruption and distractions beyond the main-focus Christian beliefs.

Daniel and I have had many conversations about faith. He is one of the most knowledgeable, intelligent, and real people I know. And he always will tell you what he thinks. Some debate because they like the debate. I don't believe that's Daniel's reasoning. He thinks logically and asks why God doesn't always show up at times and in ways that we think He would, such as to alleviate famine and suffering.

Daniel always brings up some fantastic points. We enjoy talking even when it gets heated. Our conversations always end in a hug and European cousin kisses on the cheek. Actually, I've been told by his brother, the fact that God didn't give me limbs is one reason there are questions and doubts among some in the family.

My cousin can't accept that a loving God would "leave" me, His devoted follower, without arms and legs. I've tried to explain that the Bible clearly shows that pain, sickness, disabilities, suffering, and death came in after sin was instigated by Satan himself. Our broken pieces, hurts, and shame can be turned to good by God the Redeemer. God often uses those things that once seemed terrible to help others see the true hope, joy, love, and peace we can have through Him, even amid the storms.

Daniel hasn't accepted what I accepted long ago. I will never forget the Sunday services when I wept in a backrow because his questions about God and faith would never be addressed at a local church service.

Some people won't find God in a church. I wept over Daniel's soul. I wondered, *Who will lead the army to reach those outside the church walls?* I was crying for mercy upon his life. Several of my cousins, who are like brothers to me, have not started their journey with Jesus, nor have they finished searching for truth. At least they are honest and authentic in wanting to look for truth and admit they haven't found it yet.

I will always be part of Daniel's life, and he will always be part of mine, and that goes for all my cousins, even though we may be far apart. We are family. I love and respect Daniel who has studied other religions and philosophies. He is a very knowledgeable person. I don't feel I've failed him because I haven't given up on him.

My mission is not to convert Daniel or anyone else. Instead, my mission is to love him and everyone as I encourage them to begin walking with Jesus. It's not about failing Daniel; it's actually about failing my heavenly Father when He says speak and I don't. God's love doesn't change. All I want to do is serve Him and see others set free to find their true purpose, path, and freedom.

Daniel does not believe in the supernatural or in miracles or anything that science cannot explain. He argues that there are a lot of Christians on television and in churches who mislead their listeners and followers with false hope, lies, and bad information. I have to admit this is true. Not all televangelists are bad, of course, but there are some bad ones out there, certainly.

One of my friends went into a hospital in Los Angeles with unexplained pain. Her mother in Arizona called and asked if I could go and be with this friend until the mother could get there. I found my friend in an emergency room swamped with gunshot victims. Security guards kept locking down the entire hospital because they were afraid the shooters would follow their victims there to finish them off. It was scary and real, though it seemed like a nightmare.

While we were fretting and trying to keep a low profile in the emergency waiting area during all this scary stuff, an evangelist was on television pitching a ninety-nine-dollar white cloth that was supposedly "anointed for healing." I felt like ripping the television off the wall. Scam artists and predators exist in every field, of course, but this sort of thing tarnishes all Christians and gives nonbelievers validation for rejecting God, even though His Son warned of wolves in sheep's clothing and threw the money changers out of the temple.

Atheists often cite stories about crooked clergymen when putting down Christians and their beliefs. They have long lists of grievances about Christians, including examples of televangelists who profess falsehoods and regular Christians who say one thing in church and do the opposite in their daily life. They also make the point that so many Christian denominations have doctrines that are cult-like. Many denominations even shun and deny each other's validity, claiming that only their church is the one true path to heaven.

LOGICAL DISBELIEF

Nonbelievers have many weapons to unleash in their attacks on organized religion. They are often among the most logical inhabitants of this planet. To them, it seems foolish to believe in a God you can't see. Daniel and I recently had a long talk about Christians who claim to be healers. He is very skeptical, as you might expect, even though I've told him of several healings I've witnessed that certainly were miracles to me. I don't waste time debating about ministries, but I have witnessed that God heals.

The only healing that impresses Daniel at all is my own. Doctors had told me for years that I had a degenerative spinal disease that would eventually confine me to a bed. In 2002, I had X-rays showing three holes in my spine. I began praying about this immediately, and over the years I've asked others to pray.

If you don't want to believe in miracles, that is up to you. But I can tell you that when I had X-rays taken again in 2012, there were only two holes in my spine. Two years later, X-rays detected only one hole. In 2015, the X-rays showed none. Today, after many prayers, there are no signs of that disease, though I do have a major curvature of the spine. I consider this a miracle even though some may say my spine improvements were the result of the universe or a chemistry change based on positivity or meditation.

I still have faith that my cousin will come around, and I sometimes feel I should be more in touch with those closer in my circles of relatives. They all top the list of those I want to see in heaven. Through prayer, faith, and friendship, I have hope that all my relatives will confess Jesus as Lord and walk in the strength of God.

We had another hardcore atheist in the family, my uncle Steven, who was baptized after spending most of his life denying God's existence. Everyone around him prayed for his conversion.

Many of us debated and discussed our faith with him over the years. We didn't badger him. We respected him, but we always encouraged him to keep an open mind. When he accepted Jesus Christ into his life, it was a joyous blessing—the result of the family of God doing all we could to help him walk with Jesus.

My uncle's baptism was a victory for the kingdom of God. I have devoted my life to sharing my faith on behalf of that kingdom. I am always searching for ways to open doors that will help me reach more potential converts.

BRINGING SOULS TO CHRIST

I've done so much speaking about my faith and sharing with nonbelievers that I've learned not to get emotional when they challenge me. I've had some very spirited discussions with smart and gifted debaters. There have been many times when I've prayed for God's wisdom. My goal is not necessarily to convert anyone but instead to plant seeds of faith with love and respect while provoking thought to spur them on their search for truth.

One day Jesus will return and justice will be done. This is the day when we all will know hell is real and death is real for those who've done evil or chosen not to believe in God's Word. They won't be allowed into heaven. Until then, my mission on earth is to love and know God more, love my family and neighbor, and to share my faith. God is a fair God. He will not allow His Son to come back for a second time until every person on the planet hears about Jesus. I believe we are making progress. I take hope when *The Christian Post* reports that even in Iran, where leaders of that Islamic republic persecute and imprison Christians, Open Doors USA has estimated there are as many as 450,000 practicing Christians who worship secretly in house churches.

If those believers are courageous enough to risk their lives in such a hostile environment, all Christians should be brave enough to share their faith. Atheists and non-Christians tend to think Christians believe blindly and are rigid and not open to discussions about our beliefs, so being willing to hear them out and offer your thoughts humbly and confidently can help change misperceptions and open doors. I always try to identify just where they are regarding their beliefs so I can understand their positions, listen thoughtfully, and respond wisely.

Here are some of the common questions and talking points covered in my discussions with atheists and others who question my Christian beliefs or want to understand them better.

If there is a good God, why does He allow pain in the world?

It's not God who inflicts that pain. It's the curse of sin that brought pain and suffering and death into this world. God could've stopped the serpent in the Garden of Eden, but because of free will, He did not. He could've stopped Satan, but He has chosen not to do that—yet. People may say it's unfair that God knew this would happen and allowed it.

But He made us to be His children, not angels; children who choose to believe in Him by faith and not by sight. How unfair would God be if He told us we have free will but we never heard anything other than orders from a dictating commander? Adam and Eve were given free choice; He allowed the serpent to come and tell them something different from what God had told them.

There will come a day when God will end suffering. Before that time, He calls us to help all humans hear the gospel as well as to partner with Him to alleviate suffering. Every person must be given the same choice

God gave Adam and Eve. It's not exactly clear in Scripture what happens to those who are born and die without hearing of Jesus, but we know we serve a merciful God. That gives us even more reason to do our part in reaching the world. When that day does come, there will be no more suffering and truly no pain forever. We will be with Jesus and experience His ultimate plan to be in heaven with our heavenly Father.

Until then, if you trust in Him, God will give you grace to get through anything He allows you to experience. While dealing with that pain and suffering, you have the choice to believe what God says or what others say. Those who trust in God will experience His peace through storms and strength even in the darkest nights. We have hope that no matter what happens, He will carry us through one day at a time.

Why do you think Christians are the only people allowed into heaven?

Admittedly, this is a tough one. The Bible tells us that salvation is found in no one else, because God has given no other name under heaven by which we must be saved (Acts 4:12). Jesus is not simply one way to God; He is the only way to God. He said this Himself in John 14:6: "I am the way, and the truth, and the life. No one comes to the Father except through me."

Believers and nonbelievers alike often ask me, "What happens to those who've never had a chance to know God?" Examples they give are babies who die before being baptized, the severely mentally disabled who are unable to grasp spiritual concepts, and indigenous people from primitive cultures who have never been introduced to the Bible or God's existence. Is heaven not open to them?

I honestly don't have a definitive answer to that one, and it is not my place to be the Judge. He is the one who will do that according to His will. The Bible does indicate that all babies who die will go to heaven. Babies and toddlers, like the mentally disabled, may be born with original sin, but they aren't capable of understanding the laws of God or the need to be born again and baptized. They have no concept of good or evil or any clue they need God's forgiveness.

The Bible seems to indicate that innocent children will be allowed into heaven. In Deuteronomy 1:39, in talking about children banned from the Promised Land, God says, "And as for your little ones, who you said would become a prey, and your children, who today have no knowledge of good or evil, they shall go in there. And to them I will give it, and they shall possess it."

The Bible also says that when David and Bathsheba had a baby outside of marriage and the baby died, David felt he would see the child again in heaven. "I shall go to him, but he will not return to me," he said.

Many scholars, ministers, and Bible students interpret various scriptures as indicating that God has mercy for those who die before they can be held accountable for knowing Him and seeking His forgiveness and grace. I would like to believe that, and I pray that it is true, but I can't say for certain.

There was a woman who shared with me the story about her mentally ill child who committed suicide. She asked if such children go to heaven. Again, there are questions we do not have definite answers for, and many have quoted scriptures to back their hopes. I would like to believe they are allowed into heaven. I pray that it's true. All I can do is pray for all, do my best in sharing my faith, and ask God to comfort and give peace to all His children. This is one of those times when we don't know all things but trust Him in all things.

Why is it that some atheists and nonbelievers seem to be better and more successful people than some Christians? Why would God allow that?

I don't agree that they are better and more successful people, but it's a frequent statement. Atheists and nonbelievers will often offer examples of Christians they've known who turned out to be hypocrites or even criminals who didn't live according to God's commandments. At the same time they will point to atheists or agnostics who live exemplary lives and seem to be blessed in every way. They will ask, "Why is it better to be a Christian if it doesn't guarantee you are a better and happier person?"

I do know of many people with or without religions who claim they're absolutely happy and successful. There have also been many studies that found that highly religious people visit family, volunteer, and make donations more often than less religious people. Critics of the study counter that it was flawed because it didn't include people who aren't religious at all. They contend that happiness is more often related to how well connected we are to other people and the world around us.

Actually, I think this and similar surveys miss the point. Christians are not seeking happiness in practicing their faith. They are looking for eternal salvation and a relationship with God that gives them strength, peace, and love. Without my strength in my walk with Jesus and my focus on His plan and the view of eternal life, it would be easy to be happy, sad, and depressed, then happy again based on what happens to me in this life. In contrast, when my joy is in God, others see that my circumstances, even extreme ones, are not taking away my peace and that my strength and faith remain.

I am not a Christian because of other Christians and their example. I am a Christian because I follow Jesus Christ—because of who He is and what He did in sacrificing His life for my sins, and yours. He took on the devil face to face and won. To my knowledge, no one else has done that. Jesus is the one who conquered sin and death by being absolutely God in the flesh.

My goal is to follow His example and bring as many as I can with me on that path to heaven. I can't guarantee they will all make it. I can't guarantee that all people who claim to be Christian will make it either. We all have our own battles with sin and temptation, and our ultimate measure of success and happiness is whether we enjoy life everlasting by God's side.

Why would I want to be a Christian? They don't have nearly as much fun!

This is the argument from people suffering from FOMO (fear of missing out). But what are they really missing by welcoming Jesus Christ into their lives? The response I get to that question is usually something along the lines of sex, drugs, and rock and roll. Others will say porn and alcohol or going to strip clubs.

Those earthly pursuits may deliver short-term pleasure for some, but I would argue that being a Christian offers far more in the way of long-term pleasure and happiness, not to mention eternal joy. I will concede there are some Christian denominations that can make life feel like a long, hard slog, but I also know many Christians who are happy and even joyful people without partaking in porn, strip clubs, drugs, or other vices. In fact, this applies to nearly all my Christian family members and friends. We party as hard as any group I've known, but without abusing drugs or alcohol, and we love music of all kinds. So I have no fear of missing out on anything enjoyed by nonbelievers. My Christian friends and family members understand that having a relationship with Jesus Christ is better than any earthly pleasure.

Some nonbelievers argue that having sex before and outside marriage is a pleasure that Christians typically miss out on. My response is that when you have sex outside marriage, you are toying with fire. When you have sex with someone, you join as one whether you acknowledge that or not. Outside marriage, love and true commitment are not part of the deal, and as a result someone is bound to get hurt—and it's usually the person whose heart is the most vulnerable.

Repeated sex outside marriage eventually numbs the spirit and the soul. I've had married nonbelievers tell me that their so-called open marriages allow them to have sex with anyone and, they say, it works for them. Yet most of them seem to end up divorced and lonely, from what I've observed.

Sex outside of marriage is a sin, and there are multiple scriptures on this topic. God is not a God of rules and regulations. He is the designer of everything we see and feel. Life is about using what He designed for His purposes and within His parameters so that we experience joy, fulfillment, and love.

Sex is not love itself, but it is an expression of love and sacred intimacy. Couples in marriage can enjoy each other's love and experience life as God intended. Sex is not bad in itself, but the perception has been twisted by the Enemy and turned into a lustful path to destruction.

I certainly can't speak for everyone, but as a Christian who has a personal relationship with God, I believe walking with Him each day is the deepest thrill of all. Nothing else in this world can equate to the peace and joy found in a relationship with God. It's the very reason we believe in Christian teachings. We know that nothing else can ever satisfy our thirsty souls for tangible hope, peace, and love—certainly not anything that is temporary or fabricated.

When I ask atheists to describe what makes them joyful, they often say living life to the fullest or experiencing new places, people, and things like luxury cars, boats, and other toys for grown-ups. Some say their greatest joy is having children and grandchildren, which I can certainly understand.

I bask in the happiness of life with my wife and my children, but true joy is knowing that my children are God's children too, and He will always look after them. An even greater joy each day for me is knowing that I'm closer to going home to be with Jesus, and that I will never die. Until then, I am His ambassador surrounded by angels and filled with His Holy Spirit.

Why would I want to be committed to one church and its restrictive doctrines and philosophies?

Actually, fewer and fewer Christians are members of a single denomination or church. Many, instead, are choosing nondenominational churches, and many try different churches instead of sticking with a particular church. Younger Christians, in particular, no longer tend to stay with one church over their lifetime.

Every denomination and every church has its good points and bad points, strengths and weaknesses. Those who belong to one or another usually do so because they want to belong to a community of faith and get to know the other members. Many find encouragement and enjoy growing in faith as part of a church congregation, but the trend today, particularly among younger Christians, is to check out several churches and denominations before settling into one that is welcoming and comfortable.

It's not about being committed to a church, but rather being committed to your walk with Jesus. Church is a place where you can feel comfortable to be open, talk, learn, and grow in your relationship with God. The church provides a place for asking questions, receiving counseling, and having the family of God stand by your side in prayer and support for you and your family.

There you can hear the Word of God, be fed, and grow spiritually. It does not save you, but it is critical to find a home church, be planted in it, and serve others by finding your calling and using the gifts you have been given for God's pleasure.

If you want to believe, that's fine—to each his own—but can you prove to me that God is real?

This attitude is common among nonbelievers in my homeland, Australia. They say they respect Christians but don't feel the need to give their lives to God because there is no proof of His existence.

I don't think it's the role of Christians to prove to those who don't believe that God exists. In the end, it all comes down to faith. After all, it takes a great deal of humility to admit we can't always see what truly exists.

Many atheists readily admit that no matter what evidence you might come up with, they still wouldn't be convinced that God is real. To some who demand evidence of God's existence, I use as an example who I was before and who I was after giving my life to Jesus.

My message is that He can use all of us and He has a plan. I share the stories of extreme testimonies, such as the transformation of sex slaves in India who found Jesus and came back rescuing other slaves, forgiving and washing the feet of those who once abused them. These stories have truth and power.

I rarely have anyone argue with those stories, and many ask questions to learn more. The ultimate questions for them come down to: "Are you fulfilled and happy? Do you have hope that goes even beyond this life and have peace that you will really live forever?"

That is when they say no one knows for sure if there is a spiritual realm. I then share personal stories and examples of the darkness, which include everything from demons to witchcraft and voodoo. If they only believe in science, then I tell them to investigate the occurrence of these things in remote parts of the world.

Most must decide, ultimately, whether they really want to change their beliefs. If an atheist can believe in evil supernatural powers, then logic follows that same person also must accept that there could be good supernatural powers.

Atheists often say, "I will believe when I see it." My question is, What if you found the truth about darkness first? I do not encourage them to play with such dangerous and real powers, but if we want to go the logic path, that's where discussions typically end.

Can you at least show me a sign of God's existence?

I cannot convince you that there is a God. It is only by God's grace we are even open to such a thought. Yet He knows that if He did exactly what we asked for, exactly when we wanted it, then where is the open space for needed faith?

For me it started with one step in faith, looking for the truth, and I personally have found it. In my prayer journey, I experienced the miracle of my healed spine, married, had children, and have had so many of my desires fulfilled. I have seen thirteen miracles unfold as we have prayed face to face. I have experienced real peace and strength in times I knew were beyond my power. I can point you in the direction and share what has happened to me, but in the end you are the one who has to decide to go and research, seek, and look for truth.

In addition, our entire existence is a sure sign of God's presence. Scientists have devised explanations for many things, but they've yet to explain the very beginning of it all. The world and all living things had to begin somewhere and somehow. I'm still waiting for a better explanation than that of an almighty God. Whether you are studying a strand of human DNA, watching a giraffe in the zoo, or admiring a flower in your garden, there seem to be countless examples of a Creator and Father in heaven. The ultimate designer.

It is beautiful to see God's creations. Man creates things, but how much more glorious it is to praise the One who created all of life?

How can Christians do bad things and then get forgiveness from God? It can't be that easy!

Yes, it is that easy—for us, but only because the Son of God won our forgiveness in a manner that definitely was not easy. Jesus died on the cross so our sins could be forgiven. It was hard for God to allow His Son to suffer like that. I can't imagine seeing my son on the cross, bearing the blame for all the sins of the world.

The only reason Christians can gain forgiveness on earth is because Jesus died for our sins. The wages of sin are death, and that is why no one lives forever with sin. I can't die for your sins and you can't die for mine, but I believe Jesus died for mine—and yours too. Because of His sacrifice, as soon as I take my last breath on this planet, I will arrive at the gates of heaven.

The difficult thing for many nonbelievers to grasp is that God has already offered forgiveness for every human sin. While we were still sinners, Jesus died and made that possible. He does not condemn us for our sins, but He does want us to join Him in heaven, so we have to receive God's forgiveness by repenting for our sins. If we continue to sin and refuse to repent and believe in God's goodness and love—expressed through the sacrifice of His Son, Jesus—there is no forgiveness.

So we must confess to God that we are sinners and that we want to stop living in sin, to turn away from what we know is not pleasing to God. Then true repentance—a life-changing and transforming decision—comes from the grace of God to empower us not to live for ourselves anymore but for God: to live in His plan, His way, and His strength each day.

When this is a true conversion, the fruit of that decision will show in our daily lives. God doesn't demand perfection, but by His grace He does want us to seek perfection by living according to His Word, loving Him, and believing in Him as the one true living God.

It can be hard to believe that a loving God will forgive and forget sins that you yourself can't forgive or forget. Our consciences tell us what is right and wrong, and we may be haunted by past addictions, affairs, or other sins. Often, we can't get past the memory of doing things that were selfish, greedy, prideful, or dishonest. I've known people who gave their lives to Jesus Christ only to feel depressed a few days or weeks later because they still feel guilty or remorseful for past sins. They thought that becoming a Christian would put an end to those feelings.

It doesn't work that way, but know that God forgives and forgets our sins even when we don't. He's much kinder to us than we are to ourselves, as long as we accept His forgiveness and honor and love Him. Sometimes it takes brothers and sisters in the Lord to counsel and encourage you to leave the past behind. Sometimes it's having someone pray with you and help you in your walk with Jesus. As you continue to want to serve Him and live for Him—day by day moving away from sin and evil and daily asking for forgiveness while He works in your life continually—God's grace is there for His children. You may stumble. God understands that. Just keep moving forward and praying as you go.

I will never be the perfect husband, father, son, brother, and servant of the most high God, but I strive to be righteous. I meditate on Scripture, and I spend time conversing with God. These activities help me stay closer to Him and keep me on track with His plan for my life. My family has a home church where we feel we can grow.

Remember, if you struggle with sin, don't be afraid to tell somebody and ask for help. None of us are perfect, and sometimes it takes time to break free of old habits and shackles. We all need one another, and as a family of God, we are here for one another. The cool thing about talking to a friend, family member, pastor, or a counselor is that it will encourage you and spur you to keep striving to be the best child of God you can be.

Why do Christians believe in a lot of hocus-pocus like miraculous healings, prophecies, and signs and gifts from God?

Many atheists feel that Christians decide to follow Jesus Christ, not out of faith, but because they've been manipulated to believe they will derive benefits on earth, such as healings, prophetic visions, and blessings that include good health, financial rewards, and career success. I've heard those claims from nonbelievers, and I've come across ministers and churches that cross the line by claiming that God wants them to be rich and have mansions and luxury cars.

True Christians don't love God for the gifts He might grant us. Ours is not a transactional relationship with God; it is transformational. We are transformed by our love for Him. We don't chase after prophecies or earthly goods in His name. Such things do not drive our joy or passion. Instead, we focus on our relationship with Jesus Christ each and every moment.

When I was saved and baptized, it gave me faith to begin my relationship with Jesus. It transformed me. I became a new creation. My priorities and lifestyle changed when I attained intimacy with God. It is one thing to go to church and have a superficial encounter with God. It is something altogether different to have a transformation and an ongoing relationship through daily prayer, Scripture reading, meditation, and just being present with our eyes fixed on our Father in heaven.

Psalm 37:4 says, "Delight yourself in the LORD, and he will give you the desires of your heart." Yet in a true relationship with Jesus Christ, you acknowledge and accept that God's plan for you is better than any plan you could have for yourself.

As a boy, I prayed for a miracle that would give me arms and legs. Many people still come up to me and tell me I will be healed one day. The truth is they don't know. They may want that for me, and you may pray and request it for me, but none of us will know God's plan until I take my last earthly breath.

I always pray for healings, and I have seen many appear to be healed or partially healed, including a former human trafficker in Mumbai, India, who was healed by our loving God. I tell those I pray for that there are no promises. God has a plan. We don't get what we want unless God wants it too. He may not give you what you want, but God will give you what you need, according to His plan for you. You may think you need a million dollars, but God may think you only need enough to feed your children.

The only legitimate reason for being a Christian, then, is to love God and to want what He wants for us according to His vision for our lives. If you are sick, pray for healing, and have others pray too. Pray for whatever you think you need and even the desires of your heart, but know that the greatest miracle is to know God. Learn to grow more in love with Him each day, and trust that He is in control and will bless you according to His perfect plan.

"Teach me your way, O LORD, and I will walk in your truth." I don't know if I will ever have answers to some of the questions I've received from others or those I have myself until I arrive in heaven. I know the Bible is just part of the true story. No matter how many years we search for the truth on earth, I don't think we'll find the answers to everything. Too often, those seeking the truth about God get wrapped up in a competition about doctrines and theology. Seeking the truth shouldn't be a quest for domination. Let's just get to the truth and accept it.

In the meantime, my goal is to lead as many as I can to eternal life in Jesus Christ. If I succeed in bringing only one person with me, it will be worth it. I wish that was the focus of all believers. I think we should all concentrate on what we have in common rather than fighting about our differences. The book of Acts describes the very beginning of the church as a time when all believers came together in fellowship to share meals and to pray "with glad and generous hearts, praising God and having favor with all the people" (Acts 2:46–47).

The Christian church began in private homes where the faithful gathered. Those early Christians understood that a church was not a bricks-and-mortar concept but a spiritual one. They called them house churches. In recent years, I've attended several gatherings that remind me of these early communities of faith.

I was recently in Colorado to speak at the NightVision Festival. This wasn't exactly a small house-church gathering. There were more than six thousand people there, but it did follow the apostles' model of church. We all gathered without regard to denominations or doctrines at a large park with chairs and blankets and a simple, shared intent of praising God. It was a hot and muggy night, but the atmosphere was joyful. By my count, 236 of those present accepted the Lord, and 130 rededicated their lives! Praise God!

Bringing people to Jesus is probably the biggest thrill and most rewarding aspect of my ministry. When I speak about my faith on stage, people relate to my story and the loneliness and suicidal thoughts I had. Mostly though, I believe that it's God who changes their hearts and calls them by name.

Just because I share my story doesn't mean I'm meeting everyone where they need to be met. Most nonbelievers have their own questions, like those I've listed in this chapter. I try to speak to their hearts through my own. I tell them why I didn't believe in God for a time, and then I walk them through my path to belief in our Savior, Jesus Christ.

My story is different from most, but my questions were essentially the same. I wanted to know why God created me and for what purpose. It seemed cruel to me that I had no limbs until He revealed my purpose and I saw how people responded to my story.

It took me eight years of searching to find that answer. That journey is the basis for most of my altar calls, so in delaying my answer, God helped me create my greatest gift—a story that inspires others and leads them to Jesus Christ. My story generates trust, and it helps those seeking God's light to see the path as I share what Jesus has done for me.

THE PATH TO BECOMING A CHRISTIAN

No matter what you've done, no matter how bad you've blown it, God stands ready to accept and forgive you. He is waiting for you and His door is wide open. Becoming a Christian is not about cleaning up your act and trying to become a good person. It's not some crazy sin-management system. Actually, we can never be good enough to reach God's standard of perfection. Instead, we stand before God with a bunch of broken pieces in our hands. When you hand those pieces over to Him, He can change your life!

God does all the work. God puts all the pieces of our lives back together. God is the one who makes us perfectly clean inside. God is in the business of restoring broken lives. Including yours.

To truly know God, you must say yes to Jesus. If you are ready to begin a relationship with Him, now's the time! I thought I'd end this chapter of looking at questions of faith by offering nonbelievers a summarized focus on first steps on the path to eternal life. I'm often asked how one can become a Christian, and here is my response to that welcome question. Feel free to share this with any nonbelievers searching for guidance.

First, understand and accept that you are a sinner.

The definition of sin is simple. Sin is breaking God's law. Even good people who do good things cannot please God or gain His approval. The standard in the Bible is impossibly high! None of us can reach perfection or even come close. No matter how hard you try, you can never be good enough.

The Bible says that all of us "have sinned and fall short of the glory of God" (Romans 3:23). Sin is the major roadblock between you and God. In fact, the Bible teaches that our sin is a death sentence! Romans 6:23 says, "The wages of sin is death." Heavy stuff, but that's what the Bible teaches.

Second, acknowledge that Jesus Christ died on the cross for you.

God provided the ultimate solution to our sin. You must first recognize that God's Son gave His life on your behalf. This is the good news! Romans 5:8 says, "God shows his love for us in that while we were still sinners, Christ died for us." Jesus Christ died in our place even though we deserved death. He did this so we can have true peace and enjoy a relationship with Him. He did this so that we can go to heaven and, as His children, be with Him forever with no more pain.

Third, repent of your sin.

After you admit your sinful condition, and after you acknowledge the good news of Jesus's death on your behalf, now's the time to say you're sorry.

Confess that you have done wrong, and repent of your sin. To repent means to turn away, refuse to live in a pattern of your sinful ways, and move toward God with your whole heart. Acts 3:19 says, "Repent, then, and turn to God, so that your sins may be wiped out" (NIV).

Fourth, accept Jesus Christ into your heart and life.

To be saved requires a step of belief. It requires a step of faith toward the only one who can save you. The Bible tells us that salvation is found in no one else, because no other name was given under heaven "by which we must be saved" (Acts 4:12). Jesus is not one way to God; He is the only way to God! John 14:6 says, "I am the way, and the truth, and the life. No one comes to the Father except through me."

Would you like Jesus to be Lord of your life? Are you ready to live your life in faith and obedience to Him? Then ask Jesus into your life right now. Jesus said, "Behold, I stand at the door and knock. If anyone hears my voice and opens the door, I will come in" (Revelation 3:20).

Are you ready? If you would like to begin your relationship with Christ, stop for a moment and pray. You can use your own words when you talk to God. Express your thoughts in whatever ways feel natural to you. What's most important is that your conversation with God is completely heartfelt and follows the example in the Bible: "If you confess with your mouth that Jesus is Lord and believe in your heart that God raised him from the dead, you will be saved" (Romans 10:9).

Here is a simple example of the words you might use to pray:

> Jesus, I admit that I am a sinner. I am separated from You because of my sin. But now I understand that You came and died on my behalf to completely take care of my sin problem. I am ready to repent of my sin and turn around and move toward You. I confess with these words that Jesus is my Lord and Savior. Lord, I believe You were raised from the dead for me. Thank You for saving me. Amen.

If you prayed this prayer and meant it, Jesus Christ has now come into your life! Your decision to follow Him means God has forgiven you. You will spend eternity in heaven with Him.

First John 1:9 says, "If we confess our sins, he is faithful and just to forgive us our sins and to cleanse us from all unrighteousness." And there's another encouraging verse in Psalm 103:12 that says, "As far as the east is from the west, so far does he remove our transgressions from us."

Your faith in Jesus has saved you, now go and live in peace. As Paul encourages in Romans 15:13, "May the God of hope fill you with all joy and peace in believing, so that by the power of the Holy Spirit you may abound in hope."

3

THE GOSPEL AT HOME

I came home from the office one day in the fall of 2016, and as soon as I walked in the door, I was tackled, kissed, and hugged by my two young sons. If there is a better feeling on this world, I don't know what it could be.

I'd only been home one day after being gone for two weeks, speaking in seven western European countries. My ability to recover physically from those exhausting trips seems to take longer and longer, but family hugs and kisses help me bounce back much faster emotionally and spiritually.

This was the first time Dejan, who was born August 7, 2015, was able to give me a standing hug. He's been watching Kiyoshi, who is two years older, greet me in this manner and biding his time until he had control of his little legs.

On this day, he saw Kiyoshi hug me, and he came running. He tried to pull Kiyoshi off me at first, and that sent both of them laughing and running around me as if I were their musical chair. Then Dejan halted in front and Kiyoshi stopped behind me before they both wrapped their arms around their delighted dad.

I was a single guy for too long. I'd return from long road trips to an empty house. I'd spend weeks speaking to thousands of people. They'd line up for hours to give me a hug, but I'd go home to silence and aching loneliness. I know now that God let me experience that season so I would fully appreciate the joys of being a husband and a father.

These days, more than ever, I can be the hands and feet of Jesus both on the road and at home. In sharing the gospel, my family is my first responsibility. Now when I travel, my mind often wanders to my wife and kids and home. I just want to be with them in the sanctuary of our house, where we can just be together. I love the solitude of family. I bask in their love.

I am often moved to tears when I see them cuddling and hugging each other or Kanae, who owns the hearts of her three adoring males. My wife and I had this year talked about trying for a daughter to help even the sides a bit, but we wanted to hold off for a couple more years so we could catch our breath. God had other ideas and has doubly blessed us with twin girls due to arrive soon. Be wary of those who pray a blessing of double portions for your family!

Becoming a parent for the first time—and every time—brings many surprises and revelations. By the time I found Kanae and married her, I was under the impression I had most of life figured out. Children, however, quickly dispel such illusions. They teach you that you aren't as wise, patient, energetic, and stout of heart as you might think. They humble you.

Each and every day I am forced to acknowledge that, before I had a family, I was living in a one-dimensional world. I didn't know what I didn't know, but now I learn something new every day.

Without God's wisdom, patience, energy, and strength, I don't know how any parent manages to get through each day. I have prayed more than ever in my life, seeking megadoses of all those attributes, since entering the wonderful and sometimes wild ride of parenthood.

THE WORST PAIN

I've gone public many times to confess my aversion to pain. Parenthood, however, has taught me that there is something much, much worse than my hurting—namely, one of my children in pain. Nothing makes me feel more helpless and panicked than when one of our boys cries out and we don't know what is wrong.

We were in Dallas in November 2014, visiting Kanae's mother, when our happy-go-lucky, dancing, singing twenty-month-old Kiyoshi suddenly began wailing in his bed. When we rushed to his bedside, he appeared to be suffering intense sporadic pain in a particularly worrisome part of his body.

He'd grab his pee-pee and scream for two or three seconds; then it would pass and he'd be fine. We were alarmed, of course, but we couldn't figure out what was causing his agony. We searched his clothing for something that might be sticking him or feel abrasive to no avail.

The first time this happened was around 2 a.m. We heard him cry out. We rushed in and could find no cause for his pain. Kanae stayed by his bedside and comforted him until he went back to sleep. But a few minutes later he was up and howling again.

One minute he'd be fine, and the next he was shrieking. When the episodes became more frequent—we actually timed them at every seven minutes—we took him to the emergency room. The ER doctors were mystified too. By then, the pains were occurring every three minutes. They did all kinds of tests after giving him morphine (gulp!) to ease his pain. Morphine? My baby boy?

Even then, it took eight hours to get him settled down. He was exhausted; so were his parents. I called my mum for her nurse experience. She was very concerned, but there wasn't much she could do because she and Dad were on a cruise. She cried over the fact she was not there with us at that time, but we were blessed to be in Dallas and surrounded by Kanae's family, a great source of comfort and support.

We prayed and asked everyone we knew to pray with us. We had thousands, maybe even tens of thousands, of my Facebook followers praying for Kiyoshi too. The ER doctors said their tests didn't show any problems, so we took Kiyoshi back to his grandmother's house without having any answers to the source of his outbursts. We put him in bed and had barely sat down when he started crying again. We rushed him back to the hospital where they gave him more painkillers and admitted him for the night.

SO I WILL COMFORT YOU

Our Father in heaven watched His Son suffering on earth, so I know He understands that having a child in pain is one of the worst experiences for a parent, whose every instinct is to protect and comfort the child. The scripture, "Suffer little children, and forbid them not, to come unto me: for of such is the kingdom of heaven" (KJV) kept playing out in my mind.

I prayed for God to ease Kiyoshi's pain and to guide his doctors to both a cause and a cure. I also asked for His mercy and strength. I knew God had a plan, though I had no idea what it could be. I had to trust in faith that there was a purpose greater than I could see.

Romans 5:3–4 says that we can rejoice while enduring suffering, knowing that it instills perseverance, character, and hope. First I prayed, *Lord God, stop the pain, and if You don't, please help the doctors figure out what it is so they can help him.* There was this new depth of groaning in my spirit that I had never felt before in my life. As a child, I sometimes lived in the world of the lonely because I was so different. I felt at times that my life was harder than it should have been, but this life is all about the good becoming better and, yes, at times the worst becoming worse.

The valleys do get deeper even as the mountains get higher, but between the highs and the lows is where our growth in maturity and faith occurs. Our character is forged, and we remember how faithful God has been in the past.

I think God allows us to feel weak and lost so we will be reminded that all our strength and guidance comes from Him. If life were a breeze and we were totally self-sufficient, we'd never think to ask for His help. We are supposed to depend on God so we can grow through Him and follow His path for our lives. He wants us to talk with Him and to walk with Him each day.

God sends us through seasons of good and bad so we can learn to lean on Him and to follow His Word. I spend time with God every day. I reflect and meditate more on bad days than good because I need to be drawn closer to God.

My greatest desire as a child of my heavenly Father is to know Him, grow in Him, and accept Him so He accepts me. John 15:6 says that anyone who does not accept Jesus "is thrown away like a branch and withers; and the branches are gathered, thrown into the fire, and burned." I'd rather avoid becoming kindling for a bonfire, thank you.

PARENTAL ANGST

All the prayers on Kiyoshi's behalf seemed to work because within a day the pain that had so mysteriously appeared just as mysteriously disappeared. We took him home, and he hasn't had the pain again.

Kiyoshi quickly returned to his normal happy self. In the meantime, his mother and I fretted for weeks about the source of his mysterious pain. It was our first major scare as parents, and we had trouble getting over it.

At one stage in the hospital, our tiny son had a catheter in his little body, and he was on morphine and still crying because he was hurting so badly. That's hard for a parent to get over.

They were doing blood tests. They had him drinking 250 milliliters of fluid in thirty-five minutes while he was crazed with pain. We thought it scarred him for life with all the trauma and pain. For an entire year, he freaked out whenever he saw a doctor. I know it left Kanae and me with scars of trauma that took a while to heal.

Weeks later we were still reliving it. We'd both pop up in the middle of the night, thinking we heard Kiyoshi crying, only to realize we'd dreamed it. Parents want to absorb all the pain that afflicts their children. You just want to transfer it into your own body to relieve them.

This experience gave me a small taste of what my parents must have gone through when the doctors were of little or no help to them after I was born. No one had ever seen such a child. No one had a clue what to do with me, other than to take me home and pray for the best. And they got it! (Maybe I'd better pray for more humility!)

Once my father and mum recovered from their shock, they surrendered their fear and insecurities to God. They asked for His strength and guidance, and He gave it to them. I always thought they were great parents, but now that I'm a dad myself, my respect and appreciation for them grows with each day.

GROWING FAMILY PAINS

Their example of living in faith, surrendering to God's will, and relying on the strength of the Holy Spirit gave me a powerful foundation of faith. Seeing them walk in faith also helped convince me that I could have no greater purpose than to help others accept Jesus Christ as their Savior—because there is no other strength and hope in our lives than Jesus.

I pray more now than ever before because I want to be a worthy father who reflects God's goodness and wisdom. Watching Kanae with Kiyoshi quickly became my favorite pastime. She is such a wonderful mother, so naturally giving and caring, and every day I see our son responding to her love. Their bond is incredible, and they have added so much to my life.

I was thrilled then when Kanae became pregnant again, because she has so much love to give. She again amazed us all by going through another pregnancy without experiencing any ill effects and hardly slowing down at all. Things were a little crazy just before the delivery. The person who came in to give Kanae her epidural had me worried. I thought for a moment I was in one of those television shows like *Punk'd* or *Candid Camera,* where they hide a video recorder to catch your reactions to pranks and strange events.

Around 4 a.m., this tall, skinny, and sort of clumsy guy came in. I was hit with the impression that he'd never been in a hospital before. He kept banging into stuff like a bull in the operating room. He kept picking up instruments and crashing them down, making a lot of unnecessary noise, and then he nearly tripped over tubes and wires by Kanae's bed.

Seriously, I looked around for hidden cameras, thinking someone was playing a joke on me! I didn't want to say anything that might offend him, but I was thinking, *Holy moly, is this guy an imposter?* I finally decided he must have been sleep-deprived given the late hour. I gave him the benefit of the doubt, but I was glad he wasn't in the delivery room in that condition.

TWO DIFFERENT BOYS

When Kanae first went to the hospital to have Dejan, her mother, Esmeralda, came to help me with Kiyoshi. After the birth, she stayed on to help while Kanae recovered. We were very grateful for her assistance for the month because during this period we had another major family crisis after learning of my father's cancer diagnosis. Normally, my mum and sister, Michelle, would have helped Kanae with the new baby, but of course they immediately focused on my father's illness.

Dejan proved to be an easy baby who didn't need a lot of extra attention. He has been smaller than Kiyoshi at every stage, but he never stops eating and always wants more and more, so he may catch up to his older brother one day. He is more adventurous than Kiyoshi. Our first son wasn't much for going to the beach as a baby. He didn't like the texture of the sand. Our second child runs onto the sand and then shovels it into his mouth if we don't restrain him.

Kiyoshi has always been very chill. He loves to listen to music. We think he will be either a rock star or a serious composer. He already regales strangers with stories about his vinyl music collection. Dejan is more active. He will probably be our professional skateboarder or skydiver. Don't laugh. Kanae and I have skydived together, and she did it by herself even before she knew me!

Dejan inherited our risk-taker genes. Once he was walking, we could not take our eyes off him. You let him go for a few seconds, and his hands will be in the toilet bowl or he'll be trying to get outside. He complained if he couldn't get a door open to escape us.

I used to think my father was too protective of me. Well, I've become even more protective of my sons. If I could tie them down and sit on them all day, I'd do it!

I've read that the second child learns from the first and usually hits the milestones of walking and talking earlier. That seems to be holding true. I missed out on Kiyoshi's first steps because I was traveling when he took them.

I was very grateful and deeply moved when Dejan rolled over on the ground next to me, put his hands on my chest, and stood up for the first time on his own. I wouldn't have been surprised if he'd done a victory dance, he seemed so pleased with himself.

His arrival in this world has doubled the love in my life and doubled my determination to be a good Christian, a good husband, and a good father. I quickly learned that two children seem to require ten times more work than one. In some ways, we were more prepared and less stressed because we'd been through this stage with a baby. I was struck, though, by the fact that Kanae seemed to be carrying the bulk of the load when it came to the boys.

We joke that my wife can *only* do ten or twelve things at a time. She does seem to have superpowers as a mom. She senses every need, hears every cry, and runs to the rescue whenever one of them tumbles or courts disaster. She does all this while remaining calm, cool, and collected and never complaining.

Once Esmeralda returned to Dallas, though, I could see Kanae was having trouble keeping up with both boys and all the household chores, not to mention her demanding husband. I told her she seemed to always have a baby in her arms and two monkeys running around the house—Kiyoshi and me. This worried me because I wanted to ease her burden, not add to it.

A CHILD SHALL LEAD ME

When Kanae became pregnant with our first child, I remember thinking that now I would be responsible for teaching my own son Christian values while serving as his spiritual guide. Little did I know then that my children would be teaching me so much about myself.

As parents we are quickly confronted with our weaknesses and our failings. I am so blessed to be a father, yet at the same time, I've never been so humbled. I think that, too, is part of God's plan.

Throughout my childhood and most of my teen years, I prayed for God to give me arms and legs. But I pretty much stopped thinking about my lack of limbs when Kanae came into my life. When I saw that her love for me was blind to my disabilities, I accepted myself more than ever before.

I figured if such a beautiful and caring woman could love limbless me, why mess with a good thing? I still kept shoes in my closet in case God decided to grant me a miracle, but having the love of a wonderful woman eased my mind more than anything before.

But since the birth of Dejan, I've felt the stirrings of those dormant feelings of inadequacy. I used to want limbs so I could be more independent and fit in with the majority of the human race. Now it's really because I want to pitch in with the kids. As the title of this book reflects, I do feel that as a Christian evangelist I can serve as God's hands and feet around the world. I want to do it at home, as a dad, too.

I want to represent God and faith to my children. I want to be a hands-on father as much as possible. During Dejan's first year, I often felt like I was not doing enough to help my wife. Most fathers can step in and pick up a baby or chase down a toddler on the run when their mother is busy. I wanted to do all those things but lacked the picking-up and chasing-down limbs.

Back when I was a single guy, I'd adapted so I could do most things for myself. I also had live-in caregivers who helped me with those things I couldn't do on my own. After I married, Kanae and I decided not to have live-in caregivers because it cut down on our privacy. My wife filled in whenever I needed assistance, and she was very loving and supportive. My concerns about asking too much of her were put to rest until Kiyoshi was born and suffered from colic.

This was the first time I was called out as a dad. I thought I could handle just about anything, but his screams of agony had me climbing the walls for many sleepless nights. Kanae was so much stronger, so empathetic and selfless, that I felt ashamed.

We made a rookie mistake during his illness by bringing him into bed with us to soothe him. Then he got used to sleeping with us, which wasn't a good thing. If we put him in his own bed, he'd cry and cry. We couldn't get him to sleep through the night.

Kanae never complained, but we were both like zombies from lack of sleep. I felt guilty that I couldn't get up and relieve Kanae when he was fussing and needed to be held. We did get a baby sling that I could wear around my shoulders to hold him, but Kanae had to put him in the sling, and I wasn't able to quiet him like his mother, nor could I change his diaper or bathe him.

I confess I have no tolerance for a crying baby, especially my own. It drives me mad because I can't pick up and comfort my distraught child, so I'd find myself retreating to a far-off corner where I couldn't hear the cries. Then I worried I was being a bad dad.

We eventually trained Kiyoshi to sleep in his own bed. We were just about caught up on our missed sleep when Dejan arrived and brought new challenges. I realized that when Kanae stopped to help me, she was pulled away from mothering our sons and serving their needs.

I wanted to be the dad who could help out, clear the table, put away leftovers, take out the garbage, tidy up after the boys, and take them out to play in the pool, but there are so many things I can't step in and do. Kanae was carrying the bulk of the parenting burden. In addition, we weren't getting nearly enough time together to focus on each other.

So we took measures to lighten her load and to give us more one-on-one time. We hired a housekeeper and babysitter and began going out on regular date nights to keep the relationship and our friendship strong.

I have to confess, though, that date nights were initially meant to be romantic occasions when we would look into each other's eyes and express loving thoughts, but they have turned into dinner-and-a-movie nights. We keep saying, "Next time, we'll just have dinner and talk," but then a good movie comes out, and we decide to see it instead. I promise we will work on that.

I've come to realize as a husband and a father that I need God more in my life. I am seeing more weaknesses where I wish I had strength. I need more patience, more empathy, more energy, and, yes, more sleep! But mostly I need more of God to sustain me. I do feel more stress to provide for all the needs of my family while serving my God-given purpose of inspiring and giving hope to others and bringing as many people as I can into the Christian fold.

When I was single, I never understood what couples meant when they said marriage was hard work. I thought being single was hard, and it seemed like having a loving wife would be heaven! Honestly, that's the way I feel most of the time now that I have a wife and family.

I love being married, and I am so grateful to have two healthy sons. Still, I have learned that the work of being married and having children is all about remembering to be grateful for each other and doing everything you can to keep the romance alive.

The challenge is that you can get caught up in the day-to-day demands of parenthood and adulthood. There is so much more to do and so many more demands on your time that it is easy to just react and respond until you drop with exhaustion at the end of each day.

You can't just coast along and take your relationship for granted. Resentments can build up quickly in a marriage and also in families. As parents and as a couple, we have to keep the lines of communication open, and we have to keep our faith at the forefront of our lives.

FINDING BALANCE

My day-to-day existence is more complicated than it is for most people because I lack limbs, so that is always a factor I have to deal with. I'm used to it for the most part, but I find myself resenting it more and more as our boys grow older. I definitely need God's help with that.

Like so many other mothers and fathers, I have a job too, running both my nonprofit Life Without Limbs organization, which manages my Christian outreach endeavors, and my motivational business, Attitude Is Altitude, which handles my corporate and educational speaking engagements.

We are always working on new ways to reach bigger audiences and have a greater impact with both entities. Now that I have a family, I'm very interested in using social media and technologies like webcasts so I do not have to travel so often or so far away from family.

COME ABOARD THE VUJIBUS

One blessing that we sort of stumbled upon is the VujiBus, our new, old recreational vehicle. Kanae and I had been talking for a long time about figuring out how to travel together on business and on vacations without breaking the bank. We'd been concerned about the growing expenses of traveling by air as a family. If I take my best wheelchair, which is the easiest to ride in, but not to transport, I have to reserve a seat just for it. If my caregiver comes along, that's another plane ticket both ways. So we were often having to pay for six tickets each way when traveling by plane.

We had bandied about the idea of getting a recreational vehicle big enough to carry all of us on vacation trips and even some business trips. We'd been inspired by the loaner RV provided for us for a 2015 tour. We hit nine countries in ten days on this trip, and we traveled mostly in these giant buses that were very spacious and comfortable.

We thought it would be a less expensive, less complicated mode of travel that would allow me to take Kanae and the boys on business trips and vacations. I can't drive, but we thought my caregiver could take the wheel while Kanae and I enjoyed the kids. I looked online for a used RV and quickly learned that most were out of my price range.

I'd pretty much given up on the idea when a friend told me about someone who had a 1995 RV for sale. It was well-maintained, with only seventy thousand miles on the odometer, it came with many bells and whistles, and his asking price was about half of what I'd seen elsewhere.

He gave me a great deal on this resort on wheels. To test it out we made a few short trips to Santa Barbara and Ventura. We found some great waterfront RV parks along the Pacific coast that offer views as good as any you'll find at a high-end luxury hotel.

Our biggest trip so far was into the mountains of Colorado, where we visited with friends in their wonderful cabin. When you travel by RV, you can enjoy the scenery, and on this trip we made stops in Utah, which had spectacular places to explore nature.

Diesel fuel isn't cheap, but we save the cost of airfare, hotel rooms, and even restaurants because we can bring our own food to cook on board or at campfires. It's like a vacation condo on wheels, as well as an office on wheels because I can work while the kids are sleeping.

DUAL MISSION

I pray for balance in my life because I want to serve my family as well as my Father in Heaven. My mission and ministry will never change. I will rely on the wisdom of God and walk through any open doors to share my testimony about my faith and how God has changed my life and the lives of countless others. I've also encouraged millions more as a motivational speaker, which opens more doors for me to recruit soldiers for Christ. In the first ten years of my ministry, I reached an estimated six hundred million people in locations around the world where I was permitted to talk about my faith in Jesus.

In the last ten years, that audience has doubled. I have reached an estimated 1.2 billion people across all platforms, including speaking, videos, webcasts, podcasts, Livestream events, social media, and television coverage.

I am still the highly ambitious son of my father on earth and my heavenly Father as well. My goal is to reach seven billion people with my testimony of faith in God. Yes, that is a pretty crazy goal, but we hope to keep doubling our reach every ten years thanks to the power of social media and webcasts and other national media opportunities.

My small but determined team has had to scramble more often than not over the years, but we are constantly refining our strategy. We still have huge goals, but we are using our resources more wisely.

Timing is a factor in every decision, of course. My father's unexpected cancer diagnosis has served as a reminder that every day is a blessing. Today could be our last opportunity to make a difference, to share a kindness, to hug a loved one or a stranger, or to offer a prayer of thanks.

I try to never go to bed without resolving conflicts or disagreements, especially with my wife, because there might never be another chance to tell her I love her and to ask for forgiveness. If we can't solve a problem before the lights go out, we resolve to find a way first thing in the morning. I want to say good night with peace in my heart so I can awaken to the joy of the next day, striving to be a better husband, father, and ultimately servant of God.

KEEPING IT ALL TOGETHER

I do feel overwhelmed by life from time to time with so many irons in the fire. I know I need breaks to stay healthy, but I have to-do lists and unexpected urgent matters that pop up and swallow big chunks of my time. Even when I'm supposed to be relaxing, I'm always thinking about what still needs to be done.

Work distractions take time away from family even when I am with them. I should be present for them mentally as well as physically, but my mind can wander off, and I become disengaged. This does not go unnoticed by either the boys or Kanae, and I feel badly when it happens. I need to be there for them in mind, body, and spirit.

As the Scriptures tell us, our children are a heritage from the Lord, and we need to be there for them as teachers and role models of a Christian life guided by our faith and His commandments. I pray for God's guidance. I need His help so I can be the best possible father to our children and the best possible husband to my wife.

I want to inspire them with my faith, and I want to lead them one day to life everlasting in heaven. I am in the prime of life now, and it seems like a very busy season. I'm grateful for all the blessings and opportunities, and I really feel that with God's support there are no limits on what can be accomplished as a husband, father, son, and spiritual guide.

We are thankful for a new season of greater stability in the ministry of Life Without Limbs. We are implementing plans and long-term strategies thanks to intentional systematic balances. This also gives me a whole new level of stability at home and even when I travel.

I know my children will truly appreciate the sacrifices made for the kingdom's sake. The biggest desire in my heart is to show them how much I love them by displaying my love for their mother. We will do our best to try to find the balance of teaching Scripture and showing Scripture in action. We want them to see our authentic love for God and our unconditional love for each other as husband and wife. We want to be a family grounded in the faithfulness and promises of God.

SCRIPTURES FOR PARENTING AS A CHRISTIAN ROLE MODEL

- Behold, children are a heritage from the LORD, the fruit of the womb a reward. (Psalm 127:3)
- Train up a child in the way he should go; even when he is old he will not depart from it. (Proverbs 22:6)
- Fathers, do not provoke your children to anger, but bring them up in the discipline and instruction of the Lord. (Ephesians 6:4)
- And these words that I command you today shall be on your heart. You shall teach them diligently to your children, and shall talk of them when you sit in your house, and when you walk by the way, and when you lie down, and when you rise. (Deuteronomy 6:6–7)

4

DELICIOUS FRUIT

I speak so much about my faith and how God has guided me through the challenges in my life that people often share their own stories with me. Their stories help me remember that my disabilities are nothing like the burdens so many others carry.

Xayvier Swenson's journey of faith is certainly among the most inspiring I've heard. Only someone of tremendous spiritual strength could have withstood the repeated cruelties and torment he has suffered.

Now in his early forties, Xayvier bears many scars and still faces mental health and physical challenges, but despite all he has been through, his love of God and his dedication to growing in faith are remarkable. A mutual friend introduced me to Xayvier in 2016. I could tell he was a unique character right away. He's a charming fellow and an engaging conversationalist, yet he is obviously someone who has known considerable hardship.

I was surprised that Xayvier felt the same way about me. In fact, at one point he blurted out, "You're just like me, only without arms and legs!" I believe he meant that although we have faced great challenges, we have persevered by continuously growing in faith. Even so, I have to say that Xayvier is among those Christians who inspire and humble me because the obstacles they have overcome are so much greater than anything I've had to deal with.

I've often said that growing up without a loving family is probably the greatest hardship a child can have. Xayvier never knew his father. His drug-abusing mother lost custody of him shortly after he was born. He visited her only twice as a child, and both encounters were cut short because of her drug use.

After a dozen years of silence, Xayvier's mother contacted him for help when he was eighteen years old. She was homeless and suicidal. Xayvier found her an apartment. Then he went for groceries. When he returned, his mother was shooting heroin. She overdosed and passed out. He called an ambulance. "That was the last time I saw her," he says.

As a child, he lived in more than thirty foster and group homes, most of them in Northern California. "I moved so much that sometimes I'd move to a new home, wake up the next morning, and go to sleep in a different home that night," Xayvier recalled.

Xayvier said he suffered unspeakable physical and sexual abuse during his years in the foster-care system. He was locked in closets, beaten, burned, and molested. He spent most of his childhood being terrified of attacks, sometimes from those who were supposed to be his guardians and protectors.

As a teen, Xayvier sold drugs and ran with street gangs. He had to join the military to avoid ending up in jail or prison. He enlisted in the US Army three months before the 9/11 terrorist attacks.

While training as a paratrooper and preparing for a jump, he tripped over another soldier who'd fallen while preparing to jump from the aircraft. Xayvier stumbled also, falling out of the plane, and slamming his head into the side of the aircraft. He told me he was knocked unconscious as he fell toward the landing area.

"Somehow my chute opened. If not, I'd have been a splat on the ground," he recalled. Even with his chute deployed, Xayvier had a hard landing. He suffered severe injuries to his spine, hips, and head and became hooked on painkillers from that accident and other injuries he incurred in Iraq. He was discharged after four and a half years, but his troubles, injuries, and addictions continued. He finally broke free of the painkillers, but Xayvier still struggles. After a long string of operations to mend his body, he now uses a wheelchair to get around.

Xayvier hit bottom about four years ago. He tried to commit suicide by slitting his wrists. He was rescued by a police officer who turned out to be a Christian with a heart for helping the downtrodden. The policeman told Xayvier, "I can see the Holy Spirit in you." He said God must have a bigger plan for him because Xayvier had lost nearly all the blood in his body.

I met Xayvier through Karl Monger, a veteran's advocate and cofounder of the Raider Project, a nonprofit dedicated to helping veterans make successful transitions to civilian life. Xayvier told me his dream was for the Holy Spirit to work through him in the same way God works through me.

Through all his trials and tribulations, Xayvier has hung on to his Christian faith. He faced many horrors as a child, but one of the safest places he remembers staying was a foster home run by Seventh-day Adventists who saw that he was baptized. "Ever since then, God has held my emotions and situations in check and kept me alive in circumstances where I should not have survived," he said.

Xayvier described his faith as "something planted inside me, some sort of accelerant that makes me feel lifted up and energized when spiritual people are around." He told me there have been times when he was angry with God and times when he wanted to end his life, but somehow he has managed to keep growing in faith through it all. His dream now is to help other children without parents and guidance by creating a small ministry to mentor them.

"I am building it from scratch, and people don't do something like that unless God gives them a purpose," Xayvier said. "I spent most of my childhood being terrified. Now I want to help others and show them they can persevere no matter what has happened to them."

LIVING IN FAITH REQUIRES ACTING IN FAITH

James 2:14–17 says, "What good is it, my brothers, if someone says he has faith but does not have works? Can that faith save him? If a brother or sister is poorly clothed and lacking in daily food, and one of you says to them, 'Go in peace, be warmed and filled,' without giving them the things needed for the body, what good is that? So also faith by itself, if it does not have works, is dead."

Xayvier put his faith into action to overcome challenges that might have left him angry and embittered. He admits to experiencing dark times, yet he has always chosen to follow the light of Christ. The key for Xayvier and the rest of us is to continue to grow in faith even when hard times hit. This requires doing more than praying, although prayer is certainly essential. You also have to take action to build your spiritual strength.

Don't be fooled into thinking that merely saying you are a Christian is the same as living like a Christian. In particular, don't say you love God on Sunday and then do hurtful things during the rest of the week. If you truly have faith, you treat all people with love and respect. Others can see your faith in your deeds. They see you caring for those in need, visiting the lonely, befriending the friendless, nursing the sick, and sharing whatever you have with those who have nothing.

God's three biggest blessings for me are my faith in Him, which means I want to live for Him and to know Him; then my family; and finally, my mission, which is to love God and to love my neighbors as myself. It's always about love so that people can know God loves them no matter what.

When you pray for a bad situation to turn around and it doesn't, know that God still loves you. He will carry you through. He will comfort you. You may not understand what's happening, why it's happening, or how it will ever get better, but have faith that He has a plan.

So you take one step at a time in faith, believing in something you do not see. I couldn't do that on my own; I needed to pray. I needed to ask God to comfort me. I asked God, *Teach me three things. Teach me how to pray, teach me how to thank You, and teach me how to trust You.*

When you learn how to pray, and you learn how to thank God, and you learn how to trust God, you say, *God, I don't know what You have for me today, but I'm going to trust You. This is difficult for me, but help me today.* That is the miracle: knowing that I am not alone because I have God's unconditional love. It's also knowing that God has a plan for me, that He can use even the worst parts of my life for good. Often that's when miracles happen.

That's when it doesn't matter if a storm comes, because God will give you wings to fly above the storm. And when the clouds in your storm do not part, you can still carry someone else through their storm, which is a beautiful thing. If God doesn't change your circumstance, He will change your heart, and He can make something beautiful from your broken pieces. We love God by keeping His commandments, by trying to do what He wants us to do, by loving our neighbors as ourselves (the greatest thing). You have to love yourself, though, before you can love your neighbor as yourself. You need to know the truth of your value.

Every person who comes to God is a child of God, the King of kings and the Lord of lords. Because God is the King and we're His children, this makes us not only beloved princes and princesses but also ambassadors of His kingdom and warriors in His army.

You don't need arms and legs to love God. You don't need arms and legs to love your neighbor as yourself. And you don't need arms and legs to stand in front of the gates of hell and redirect traffic.

IF YOU DON'T GROW IN FAITH, YOU SHRINK IN IT

You may not be aware of it, but people who are seeking faith will watch and take note of how you respond to life's toughest times. They observe how you love and treat others. They judge your authenticity by how you handle yourself and whether you live up to your claims when the dark days descend.

Living as a Christian in the modern world requires continuously seeking God's wisdom and support throughout our lifetimes and especially in times of struggle and despair. When I gave my life to Jesus Christ as a teenager, after years of doubt and questioning God's will, I accepted Him as my hope. I believe you have to keep growing in faith by feeding your spirit with the Word of God. This renews our minds and gives us the courage to do what He wants us to do.

When you refuse to abandon your spiritual beliefs, you demonstrate that you love God and want to serve Him. Our flesh is weak. We are easily distracted. Yet we need to spend time with God each day. He won't open our Bibles for us, but God wants us to read His Word daily.

This is one way to keep growing as a Christian. I know I can read a Bible chapter six straight days and learn or experience something new each time. God wants us to meditate on Scripture so we can apply His lessons to our daily lives.

When I was a teenager, I learned about nine qualities—the fruit of the Spirit—that help us to keep growing in faith. The apostle Paul named the fruit of the Spirit in Galatians 5:22–23: "But the fruit of the Spirit is love, joy, peace, patience, kindness, goodness, faithfulness, gentleness, self-control."

We were taught that when our actions are guided by all these qualities, we show the world that we have given up selfish ways and sinful desires. When our daily lives are marked by love, joy, peace, patience, kindness, goodness, faithfulness, gentleness, and self-control, we demonstrate that the Holy Spirit is working through us because we have turned our lives over to Jesus Christ.

You can't do anything good without God. That's the beautiful thing: because God is love, and with the love of God, I love, too. God gives me His fruit of the Spirit, and because God loves me, it gives me meaning and purpose. The nine fruits are part of God's divine nature, and they come from His Holy Spirit. Let's look at each one and how we can apply it to our character and our journey of faith.

LOVE YOUR NEIGHBOR

When I began speaking to church youth groups as a teenager, I often spoke about the nine fruits of the Holy Spirit, incorporating them into my speeches just as I've worked to incorporate them into my life. For example, when I began telling teens in my audiences that I loved them unconditionally, just as God loves them, the impact was beyond anything I had expected.

Girls, boys, teachers, parents—it didn't matter, they all grew teary-eyed. Some wept openly, even big, tough guys! Then they'd line up after my talks to give me hugs. I'm always surprised and grateful when teens are eager to hug me. They remind me how much we all want to be loved and appreciated.

Many people have aching hearts because they've never been told they are loved. My parents told me nearly every day they loved me. I never realized what a gift that was until I told others the same thing. Many said they'd never been told that. They were so grateful.

Jesus told us we must love God before we can truly love one another, which is the greatest commandment. We show our love for God by reading the Bible and then living accordingly, which means treating everyone with kindness and compassion, even those who don't like us and try to hurt us.

We can demonstrate our love for God and each other by reaching out to those in need. Feeding the hungry and caring for the sick are major acts of love, but even being willing to listen or spend time with someone who is lonely is an act of Christian service.

THAT YOUR JOY MAY BE FULL

Watching my sons play is one of my greatest pleasures. I once thought it was a parent's role to teach his children, but now that I'm a father, I understand I have much to learn from them. One of the lessons they've taught me is that we are born with joy in our hearts. I see it in their playfulness and in the ways they express their love for each other and their mother and, yes, even their dad. Lucky me!

The challenge we face as we grow into adults is to retain that joy in our hearts. Faith is the key to doing just that! In fact, my faith has given me access to levels of joy I likely never would have experienced without Jesus Christ as my Savior.

My parents had expected to feel joyful at the birth of their first child, but instead they were shocked when I was born without limbs. They experienced grief, fear, guilt, and worry instead of the usual happiness because they didn't know how to raise a child with such severe disabilities.

Their initial negative reactions eventually turned more positive when they saw my joyful spirit unfold as I grew. God didn't give me limbs, but he did instill in me an unstoppable belief that I could do anything. In my innocence, I took life as it was presented to me. I lacked arms and legs, but I did not lack the innate ability to embrace opportunities and adventures.

Certainly, I had to adapt to living in a world that expected each of us to have all our limbs, but with the help of my family, I surpassed all expectations and overcame my limitations. Only later, as I entered adolescence, was I made aware of my shortcomings, my "different" body, and the fact I would never play professional soccer or do so many other normal things.

Those realizations did take some wind out of my sails initially, but my joy returned when I realized God created me to inspire and give hope to others. When I began traveling around the world to do that, one of the most amazing revelations was that there is joy even in the poorest, neediest, most desperate corners of the world.

In Mumbai, Africa, and other places, I saw boys and girls laughing and dancing in orphanages, ghettos, and barrios. They taught me that joy comes from within, and for Christians it comes from faith in God and belief in life everlasting by His side.

I'm convinced that those who follow Jesus will find a deeply rooted contentment, the kind that allows you to sleep well at night, knowing your focus is on the one who never changes and remains the same even when your own circumstances are in turmoil. I have learned that if I focus on Jesus and on serving others, my happiness cannot be quelled.

If your heart is bogged down by events and situations beyond your control, don't give in to the burden. Instead, ask God to restore your joy. When we make Jesus the priority in our lives, there is nothing we can't overcome. Nehemiah says, "the joy of the LORD is your strength."

When my life is down in a valley, as it has been many times recently, I call to mind Psalm 64:10, "Rejoice in the LORD and take refuge in him." If that doesn't lift my spirits, my next move is to reach out to trigger joy in the lives of others. Lifting the spirits of another person often lifts mine. Even if I still struggle, I know that I've put my faith into action and eventually it will bear fruit.

BLESSED ARE THE PEACEMAKERS

With recent challenges in my life, I was reminded that the only true peace is found when you have a relationship with Jesus Christ. Only He can protect and guide you through the worst of times. The only way to lasting peace is through God. Scripture tells us "[God] himself is our peace."

Jesus said the same thing shortly before He died on the cross when He told His followers, "I have said these things to you, that in me you may have peace. In the world you will have tribulation. But take heart; I have overcome the world."

I didn't have peace in my spirit until I let God into my heart. To hold on to that peace and to always be able to access it requires praying throughout each and every day so I continue to grow in faith and serve as a Christian role model. God's peace—knowing that He is there for us, knowing that I can draw from His strength, and knowing that everlasting life in heaven awaits me—is often the only thing that gets me through times of darkness and despair.

In my podcast on peace, I talk about one of my favorite hymns, "It Is Well with My Soul," which was written in 1873 by lawyer Horatio Spafford after his four daughters died in a transatlantic shipwreck. He actually wrote the lyrics while sailing to England to retrieve their bodies, which is one of the saddest things I can imagine. Yet Spafford was able to find peace through his faith, as he expressed in his hymn.

> When peace, like a river, attendeth my way,
> When sorrows like sea billows roll;
> Whatever my lot, Thou hast taught me to say,
> It is well, it is well with my soul.

Whenever I need peace because something is shaking up my world, I think of those words, "It is well with my soul," and I immediately feel peace. The words remind me that, because I know Jesus, His spirit resides in me and His peace is mine to claim. I encourage you to remember that when you are in need of peace in your life.

PATIENCE BEARS FRUIT

Kanae grew up working with her father, who was in the nursery and landscaping business and later started a fish-breeding business so he could spend more time at home. Her late father, Kiyoshi, the namesake of our first child, came to Mexico in his job as an expert in agriculture. He met her mother, Esmeralda, at a Japanese-owned nursery where she worked as a secretary.

My wife, then, has gardening skills in her DNA. She has two green thumbs! She created and now nurtures a huge hillside garden behind our house where she grows all kinds of flowers and plants, as well as vegetables and fruit of every variety. I am in awe of her patience in the garden. She plants seeds and then waters them daily, waiting for the sun to nourish them and bring the plants out of the soil.

Her gardening reminds me that I have to be patient in my own work as I plant seeds of faith and wait for them to grow. I pray that those seeds will be nurtured in the millions of people around the world who've attended my speeches and watched my videos.

I wasn't born with much patience, but since I've become a husband and father, I've definitely had to acquire it. When our first son was born, a longtime friend told me, "Now you will have to hurry up and learn patience!" He was being funny but also truthful. I'd been a single guy a long time, and Kanae and I had only been married a year before Kiyoshi was born. Having a baby teaches you very quickly that the world no longer revolves around your wife and you. Everything revolves around the baby and the baby's needs.

That is a very valuable lesson to learn, because patience doesn't come naturally to most of us. It takes a certain level of maturity to accept that sometimes our selfish needs aren't the world's priority. I struggle with this reality, as do most people. Our patience is tested each day, whether it's standing in line for coffee at Starbucks, being stuck in a traffic jam, or waiting for water to boil or paint to dry.

God tells us that love is patient. If we work to master patience over our lifetime, we reap many benefits, including less stress on our bodies and our relationships. We also become more like God, whose patience with us knows no bounds. The apostle Peter says, "The Lord is not slow to fulfill his promise as some count slowness, but is patient toward you, not wishing that any should perish, but that all should reach repentance" (2 Peter 3:9).

God is holding back on the end of life on earth because He doesn't want anyone to be lost on the day of reckoning. He is giving everyone space and time to accept Jesus Christ as their Lord and Savior. The next time you catch yourself overreacting or lashing out because you've lost patience, remember that God is patient with you, waiting for you to become the best Christian you can be.

I pray for patience in my own growth as a Christian and as one who wants to escort as many souls to heaven as I possibly can. Jesus tells us in the parable of the sower (Luke 8:15): "As for that in the good soil, they are those who, hearing the word, hold it fast in an honest and good heart, and bear fruit with patience."

Patience is both a gift from God and a virtue. Rest in the knowledge that God's timing for events is perfect. I believe that when you surrender your life in full, with complete trust and patience, there is another great reward that comes your way: God's strength.

James 1:2-4 says, "Consider it pure joy, my brothers, whenever you face trials of many kinds, because you know that the testing of your faith develops perseverance. Perseverance must finish its work so that you may be mature and complete, not lacking anything." (NIV). We all face trials, but it helps to remember that God has amazing plans we cannot see.

LOVE IS PATIENT AND KIND

Offering kindness to others is one of the simplest ways to serve as a Christian role model and inspire others to give their lives to Jesus Christ. Scripture is quite clear on this, as in Ephesians 4:32: "Be kind to one another, tenderhearted, forgiving one another, as God in Christ forgave you."

Sadly, there are many like my friend Xayvier who grow up in this world without receiving much kindness. I've met far too many teens and adults who grew up in violent homes, in orphanages, and even on the streets. To me, those who lack kindness in their lives are burdened more severely than I am with my lack of limbs. I can't imagine growing up without loving parents.

Those who have never known kindness are most in need of it, yet all too often they reject it. They are driven and controlled by anger and hurt. They often become bullies, predators, and abusers themselves. They don't feel valued, so they see no value in the lives of those around them.

As Christians, we should love them anyway. In fact, we should love them all the more because their need for our kindness and understanding is so great. We should love them in spite of their hostility. We can be a miracle for them. We can turn their lives around by showing that we value them. We can look past their circumstances and inspire them to do the same.

Mother Teresa is probably the most famous missionary to embrace the poor and downtrodden, leading them to love Jesus through her acts of kindness and caring in the slums of Calcutta. All of us can learn from her example. You can have an impact anywhere: in your neighborhood, your school, your community. Look for those who need your kindness. Be kind and compassionate just as God is to all of us.

I've seen it work in the poorest and cruelest environments. I've met with sex slaves in Mumbai and witnessed their compassion for each other. I've seen how they respond to kindness and how it feeds their hungry souls.

This is evidence that God is at work: seeing those who've never known kindness show it to others. If you haven't known love, how do you show love? I believe kindness exists in all of us, but it has to be nurtured to come alive. Faith can do that too. In fact, to grow in faith, we must practice kindness and compassion.

God loves us unconditionally, even when we are sinful and don't deserve to be loved. As Christians, we need to reflect God's love and kindness to others. That is one of the best ways to serve as a role model for those who are still trying to find the path to Jesus Christ.

I've heard some people mistake kindness for a sign of weakness. In truth, it takes great strength of faith and character, as well as great humility, to be kind to those who may not seem to deserve it. So fear not; follow the example of Jesus and arm yourself with love and kindness. Plant seeds of love. Give a free hug or a smile to someone each day. You may bring about a miraculous transformation, turning a bully into a friend or a friend into a follower of Jesus.

I WILL MAKE ALL MY GOODNESS PASS BEFORE YOU

It's no secret there was a time in my life when I found it difficult to understand the goodness of God. I could not fathom why a kind and compassionate Creator would bring me into the world without arms or legs. My parents admit they struggled at first with this question too.

None of us had an inkling that one day millions of people would come to see me as an earthly example of God's goodness. I'm not saying I'm anything special. I am just a man like any other man, except for a few missing bits and pieces. I serve as a reflection of His grace only because He uses me for His purpose—to bring hope and faith to others.

As a boy, I did not understand how a good God could allow my parents and me to experience grief and hardship because of my disability. We all prayed that God would fix me. We did not understand that, in God's eyes, I was never broken. I was His perfectly imperfect creation and well suited to doing His work in a perfect world made imperfect by original sin.

Part of the problem is that we tend to think of goodness as happiness and joy. God's definition of goodness is more about living according to His commandments. My mum and dad used to always tell me I needed to be "a good little boy." It's always been a goal, but too often I fall short of being as good as I can be, even now as a man. The fact is that true goodness doesn't come naturally to mere mortals. We are flawed beings in all ways, including spiritually. Sinners all, we fight the battle each and every day.

We need the Holy Spirit within us and God's strength as our shield against sin. Otherwise we are helpless. Psalm 53 says no one does good, not even one of us. True goodness results from our relationship with God. If you invite Him to forgive your sins each day and each night, you will continue to grow in faith and favor. He will perfect His work in you, and that is what it means to be good.

I began to grow in faith when I accepted that what I once considered a cruel burden could be a blessing because my unique appearance draws people to me. I now know that instead of being disabled, I am, in fact, enabled to serve His purpose. As the psalm says, "No good thing does he withhold from those who walk uprightly."

Yes, the nearness of God is good! When we walk in faith and go by faith, we put a *Go* in front of disable, and it spells "God is able." Ephesians 3:20–21 says He "is able to do far more abundantly than all that we ask or think, according to the power at work within us."

A GOOD AND FAITHFUL SERVANT

You and I can always hold on to hope because we worship a good and faithful Father in heaven. God is always faithful to us, but what about our faithfulness to Him? True faith means walking on God's path at all times and not straying or being lured off by fleeting temptations and distractions.

We may not always feel that Jesus loves us or that God is good—especially when we hit hard times or major challenges—but we have to remain faithful, knowing that God is good and He has our best interests at heart even when we don't understand what they might be. Life's ups and downs are tests of our faith. We can't abandon God when things turn bad or forget to pray to Him when things are going well, not if we expect God to be faithful to us at all times.

I don't think God would have sent me around the world to speak to millions of people if I wasn't faithful to Him. Now, God didn't allow that to happen on my time schedule. He allowed it to happen only when He knew I was ready by His grace.

Before I could run as a speaker, He made sure I knew how to walk. God sent me to speak in front of youth groups and middle schoolers to prepare me for packed arenas and megachurches. We take steps of faithfulness, and if we stay strong, God continues to guide us.

We may think God is not there when things don't go the way we want them to go. We may feel abandoned if He doesn't seem to be coming through for us. Yet in those times of doubt, we need to grow our faith and pray to Him even more. We need to remember Philippians 4:19: "And my God will supply every need of yours according to his riches in glory in Christ Jesus."

This doesn't say "some," "a few," or "only the really important" needs. God promises to meet *all* our needs. He knows when we need them. He never comes early. He never arrives late. He always shows up at just the right time to meet the right need.

We don't have to be anxious about our todays or tomorrows. We can bring our deepest needs to God and trust He will come through for us. Our goal should be to come through for Him with the same faithfulness that grows with each passing day until we meet Him in heaven. Ask God to help you be faithful in all your relationships, and thank Him for being faithful to you.

Faithfulness is a sign you are filled with God's Spirit. My prayer is that when I do see Him face to face, God will say to me, "Well done, My good and faithful servant." In the meantime, my prayer for you is that you experience and hold on to His peace. That you will remember to "not be anxious about anything, but in everything by prayer and supplication with thanksgiving let your requests be made known to God. And the peace of God, which surpasses all understanding, will guard your hearts and your minds in Christ Jesus" (Philippians 4:6–7). Know that this peace is real—when you do not get a miracle, He can still use you to be one.

LET YOUR GENTLE SPIRIT BE KNOWN TO ALL MEN

Gentleness is all too rare in today's world, where bullying, brashness, and hyper-competitiveness are all too common. The fruit of gentleness necessary for growth in faith isn't about social graces as much as it is about graciousness under pressure.

Have you ever seen someone silence a critic with a gentle word? Jesus, who said, "I am gentle and humble in heart," was known for showing quiet strength in the face of critics and captors. Followers were drawn to Jesus because of His gentle manner and quiet strength. His interrogators were stunned when Jesus did not lash out at their accusations. Even while being tortured and dying on the cross, He asked God to forgive His tormentors.

This gentle strength works for mere mortals too. Nelson Mandela earned the respect of his jailers, won his freedom, and became the leader of his nation by using gentleness to disarm the hatred of his persecutors. There is power in gentleness. It can soothe and heal in so many aspects of life.

When we choose a gentle approach, we create a safe, nonthreatening environment around us. I was reminded of that when Xayvier told me of his experiences with Lifesavers Wild Horse Rescue, which offers a healing program for combat veterans with post-traumatic stress disorder.

Xayvier was going through a rough period when he entered this program. He'd shut himself off from most people. He was bitter and angry. Then he found himself in a small pen with a wild horse, and as he said later, "Something switched on."

Xayvier instinctively realized the wary wild horse would not respond well to him if he continued to be angry and anxious. So he went deeper, tapped into the well of faith inside, calmed himself, and offered a gentle presence to the mustang. The horse immediately settled down and, for the first time, approached him without fear or hostility.

In 1 Timothy 6:11, we are encouraged to "pursue righteousness, godliness, faith, love, steadfastness, gentleness." That is the way to continue to grow in faith. To counter cruelty and bullying, pursue gentleness and you will attract gentleness. Know, as Jesus did, "a soft answer turns away wrath."

"GENTLENESS, SELF-CONTROL: AGAINST SUCH THINGS THERE IS NO LAW"

When Xayvier calmed his own spirit to gentle the wild horse, he practiced self-control, which, according to Scripture, is the final fruit necessary for continuous growth as a Christian. This is an essential quality, but it's one we are born without. As infants, our survival instincts dominate, and we are selfish in our demands for food and comfort. I love my sons, but when they were babies, Kanae and I would have appreciated if they'd allowed us to sleep through the night instead of crying out when they needed something.

They couldn't not cry, because they hadn't learned self-control. Sadly, some people don't ever seem to learn it. They are unable to control their worst impulses, whether it is for more food than they need, drugs, alcohol, or other false pleasures and addictions.

Most of us learn to harness and control self-destructive impulses and urges, but it's not always easy. We need God's help. He gave us the Holy Spirit to live within us and give us the strength to stay on the path to spiritual fulfillment instead of straying into self-indulgence. Scripture quotes the apostle Paul: "God gave us a spirit not of fear but of power and love and self-control."

The fruit of self-control is essential for helping us avoid falling into temptation, as well as for helping us be strong enough to stand and proclaim our faith so others may find everlasting life in heaven.

5

OUT OF THE BOX

I met my friend and caregiver Peter and his wife, Isabel, at a prayer gathering in California six years ago. They are about my age, and they'd been married just three years when they became foster parents. That was six years ago. Since then they've had nineteen foster children stay with them for various periods. In 2016, they adopted one of their foster children, Nathan, who was then just eighteen months old.

Through this caring couple and others, I've learned that foster parenting is one of many ways Christians can put their faith in action to bring more of God's lost children to His kingdom. I am in awe of my friends and all those who serve as foster and adoptive parents. Theirs is a special calling and a mission like no other. They are truly doing God's work and following the path of Jesus on earth to encourage faith and bring hope to those who otherwise might never know a safe and loving home or their Father in heaven.

When most of us think about sharing our Christian faith, we think of serving as pastors, church leaders, missionaries, or volunteers who offer their testimony. In this chapter I want to explore some out-of-the-box paths for sharing and encouraging our Christian faith that many might not think of but perhaps should consider because they can have such a tremendous impact. Mostly, I want to open your mind to greater possibilities for practicing and growing your faith.

Foster care saves lives by rescuing the neediest children, those who have been abused, abandoned, or neglected. This may be one of the highest forms of Christian service and faith sharing because foster parents help to break generational cycles of abuse and neglect, making the world a better place for decades to come. One child saved from a life of despair can result in saving hundreds more in future generations.

Christianity Today cited a report from the Barna Group, a research organization focused on faith and culture, that said 31 percent of Christians have seriously considered foster parenting compared to just 11 percent of non-Christians, but only 3 percent of those Christians have actually become foster parents. The study found that many Christians who have considered foster parenting or adoption have backed away because of fears that it is too much work, expensive, dangerous, or heartbreaking.*

Peter and Isabel are very candid about their experiences. They say foster parenting does call for hard work and even occasional heartbreak when a child they've bonded with moves on to another location or adoption. Yet they also said it was the perfect mission for them, and they encourage other young Christian couples to open their hearts and homes in this special outreach.

They initially learned about the need for foster parents while considering adoption. After they'd been married a couple of years, Isabel had a miscarriage, always a tragic event, and then could not become pregnant.

* Jamie Calloway-Hanauer, "Mythbusting for Foster Parents," *Christianity Today,* June 2014, www.christianitytoday.com/women/2014/june/mythbusting-for-foster-parents.html.

They first tried to adopt twin girls, but the process did not go well. A lengthy application-and-approval procedure lasted seven months, and then at the last moment the children's great-grandmother stepped in and claimed them.

After that emotionally wrenching experience, Isabel and Peter became wary of adoption. They had both dreamed of having many children, so they decided to try foster care as an alternative, seeing it as a God-given calling. They thought saving children from neglect and abuse and sharing Scripture with them, along with giving them a loving, supportive, and faith-filled upbringing, would be doing His work.

Peter and Isabel learned that most children in foster care have suffered abuse of some kind, and such children often grow into abusive adults and parents themselves unless they are provided with a loving, nurturing environment to break the abusive generational cycle. The first foster children Peter and Isabel cared for were a challenge, but it did not deter these two humble servants. In fact, they became even more convinced that God had called them to serve a great need. These children had been rescued from a child-pornography ring. They had been abused in some of the worst possible ways and were suffering severe emotional and psychological problems.

They now have a fourth child and are trying to adopt. The children's ages are eighteen months, six years, nine years, and thirteen years. Each of them has issues that require great love, patience, and God's strength.

One of the children (we'll call her Faith) was four years old when my friends accepted her as a foster child. She had been living on the streets or in a car with her homeless mother. She was tough and hardened beyond her years. Upon her arrival, Faith announced that she did not want to be with Peter and Isabel, even though they provided a much safer and more comfortable environment.

Peter quickly became concerned that the child was being tormented by the devil. On her first night with them, Faith threw herself against the wall and then twirled around, gagging and picking a scab off her skin. She cursed like an adult and used terrible, foul language. She rejected any attempt to hug or soothe her; she fought and screamed until they left her alone.

Peter and Isabel prayed for her, asking God to bring her peace.

"Whatever she had been exposed to had traumatized her," Peter said.

Faith's meltdowns were a serious problem. Isabel had to pull the car over once, because Faith was throwing a severe tantrum. On another occasion, at her preschool, Faith threatened a teacher with a pair of scissors and chased her around the classroom. School officials had to shut down the school and call the police to get Faith under control.

"She only knew violence. That was how she communicated," said Peter. "We found it so hard to communicate with her or to help her feel protected and loved. I prayed and the Lord told me to love her, embrace her, and show her I cared about her. Isabel and I had to rally around her because she had never been exposed to love or even attention."

Over several months, they slowly won the trust of the wary, wild child. They needed all of God's strength and the help of professional counselors and teachers specializing in severely traumatized children with behavioral challenges.

"Seeing that little girl come to light has been just an incredible blessing," said Peter.

COMING TO THE LIGHT

As Faith accepted their love and support, my friends introduced her to the Bible, and the results were quite remarkable considering their initial battles with her. One night, while having a backyard cookout, Faith asked her foster father, "Do you want to know what Jesus looks like?"

"Sure, tell me, sweetie," he said.

"His eyes are as bright as the sun, like flames of fire, and Jesus wears a beautiful man dress with a ribbon across his chest. His face is very beautiful," she said.

"Really?" said Peter.

"And do you want to know something else, Papa?" the child continued. "Jesus is standing right here in our backyard!"

"Where is He?" Peter asked.

"Right there," said the child, pointing to a spot.

Peter dropped his fork in amazement, and then quietly said a prayer with his wife and foster children. If this little girl had a vision of Jesus, it was a miracle. But even without a vision, the fact that she had come so far so quickly in her journey of faith was astounding to her foster parents.

Peter reported that Faith has a long, difficult road ahead as she grows and becomes more aware of the abuse and neglect she suffered as a child. But thanks to my friends and their work on God's behalf, this child now walks with Jesus in her heart.

"She started singing this song about Jesus coming back soon while riding on a cloud with many angels," Peter said. "I asked her Sunday school teacher if she'd taught Faith that song, and she said no. Then I asked Faith, and she said, 'Jesus taught it to me.'"

Peter believes Faith will learn to draw upon God's strength now that the seeds have been planted. She may even rejoin her mother and her eight siblings one day. "We had thought that Faith might be placed with us permanently, but the Lord worked with her mom and got her sober. She is back on her two feet, and we pray for her and meet with her regularly. So we will see how it unfolds," he said.

The volatile child who once cursed her foster parents now calls her foster father Papa Pete. He bought her an inscribed necklace: "You will forever be my princess and God's as well."

Faith now has a foundation on which she can build a life, and that is the greatest gift a foster parent can give.

REACHING AND TEACHING

Foster parenting requires tremendous patience, empathy, understanding, and faith, but it can be one of the most rewarding ways for a Christian couple to serve as the hands and feet of God. They are bringing His most needy children back to His flock and helping them become responsible, productive, faith-filled adults with the opportunity for everlasting life in heaven.

Many children in foster care have never had a chance to know God because of emotional and behavioral problems or learning impairments. Peter and Isabel tried early on to teach Bible classes using videos and picture books, but their kids had a hard time following those teaching tools. They eventually came up with the idea of using action figures to stage Bible stories such as David and Goliath, and that has seemed to work. You have to admire their patience, creativity, and dedication.

Honestly, many of Peter's stories about the challenges of foster parenting are difficult to hear because of the intense emotional pain and suffering their foster children have endured. The couple's dream is to one day have a working farm where they can create a safe haven. There they hope to raise foster and adopted children while giving these kids the love they have never known. In this nurturing environment, they can also teach and model foundational life lessons and the spiritual guidance the children need to make it as adults.

"I told my thirteen-year-old recently that my biggest hope for him is that he will continue to always hold on to God," Peter said.

Peter and Isabel are exceptional people. They have made great sacrifices to do God's work on earth.

SERVING A GROWING NEED

There are more than 420,000 children in foster care nationwide, and many of them are in need of permanent homes.* Some of them, because of their histories of abuse and neglect, require so much special attention that it's unlikely they will ever find permanent placement with a family.

Nationally, there are fewer and fewer couples willing to serve as foster parents. For that reason, the trend in foster care is toward group homes that are run like institutions. There are children with histories of violence and criminal behavior who may be served best in a tightly controlled environment, at least for the short term, but no one thinks it is the most beneficial place for the long-term health and welfare of young people in need of love and compassion.

My friends signed up as foster parents fully aware that the children who'd be placed in their care would bring challenges. They did not expect that other parents and individuals in their families and community would have issues with their mission to save these lost kids. Peter and Isabel, who are Hispanic, said some have criticized them for taking in African American children, claiming they should serve their own needy kids first.

"We hunker down with what the Lord has placed in our hearts," said Peter. "God is the Father of the fatherless. The criticism has been eye-opening, but it doesn't move us from our position to do what we are supposed to do."

Peter and Isabel attempt to bring young people to Jesus Christ through their dedication and service. By law, they cannot demand that their foster kids attend church or force them to read the Bible, and that is understandable. My friends and I agree it is better to lead through example and to simply serve as guides and mentors who, with God's grace, open the door

* Children's Rights, New York, www.childrensrights.org/newsroom/fact-sheets/foster-care.

and introduce the children to better lives and even the eternal happiness awaiting them.

PLANTING SEEDS

This is doing God's work at the most personal level. One of Peter and Isabel's foster children was a streetwise thirteen-year-old boy who at first felt their demonstrations of faith through prayer, service, and church attendance were just plain weird.

"We were feeding the homeless, and he asked, 'Why do you care for these people?' " Peter recalled. "He had a lot of questions, which is good. I could tell he was really seeking to understand rather than just dismiss our desire to follow the path of Jesus."

The teen's position at first was that the homeless were just bums. Peter told him that as Christians they felt called to serve those in need without judging why they were needy. He then told him the story of Jesus's feeding the multitudes with loaves and fishes. He explained that they were following the example of Jesus by feeding the hungry.

"You may think it doesn't make a difference, but some of these people haven't had a decent meal for days, and they will always remember the Christian dude who came to them when they were hungry," Peter told his foster son.

In these subtle ways, Peter and Isabel plant the seeds of faith and pray that God will nurture them so they will bear fruit.

"The Lord directs me to do prayer and show faith in God," Peter said. "Sharing is the most important part."

A JOURNEY OF RESTORATION

As Peter often tells me, foster parenting is where spiritual beliefs are tested against raw realities. A twelve-year-old girl rescued from a prostitution ring is not an easy lost soul to lead to Christ. But again, that makes the victories all the more rewarding for Christian foster parents.

"This girl had no hope after being forced into prostitution, but over the course of a year, we walked with her on her journey of restoration," Peter said. "The Lord restored her identity. She was able to get with God. A relative later adopted her, but we still hear from her, and she is doing well and reading her Bible and praying.

Remember that Proverbs 22:6 tells us, "Train up a child in the way he should go; even when he is old he will not depart from it." I think that is the gift that foster parents give to these children, and when they continue on God's path, that is the gift these children give to their foster parents. "We are always happy to see kids reunited with family in the right situations, and when we see that they go with God and continue to flourish, well, that is what we truly love," Peter said.

This compassionate man understands the attitudes as well as the needs of lost children because he had boyhood friends who were in foster-care group homes. Many of them were runaways who had fled foster homes after their parents abandoned or lost custody of them. He saw that those who never knew permanent homes ended up addicted to drugs, violence, and imprisonment.

Peter's mother abandoned him when he was thirteen. He had very little supervision. He'd gone to a Christian church as a young boy, but he lost his spiritual and moral bearings for nine years. He recalled that some of the boys from his childhood church were in good foster homes. They were much happier than those who were in group homes or still on the street.

"I saw the difference in them, and I was exposed to their realm of life," he said. "I remember, at an early age, I told my mom that one day I wanted to have a house with a lot of kids who needed better lives."

Once foster children become acclimated in their home, accepting the rules of the house as well as the love and compassion of Peter and Isabel, they often begin to appreciate the everyday aspects of a family life. Recently one of the boys in his care asked Peter if they could have a family barbecue. It was a small thing, but something this boy had never experienced. The joy that such a simple custom brought to his foster son once again confirmed Peter's belief that they were doing God's work. "All he wanted was a barbecue, and it was such a blessing to provide it for him," said Peter.

Still, couples who wish to do God's work as foster parents may hesitate. Foster kids are stigmatized because so many come from troubled backgrounds. Peter often hears from prospective foster parents that they are afraid to take in children with challenges, but he counsels them that with patience and love and the help of the Lord, miraculous transformations can occur.

"It's challenging but so rewarding once a child opens his heart. At first you see behavior that reflects what they've been through. But with time you see what God has placed in them. These kids didn't choose to be born to drug addicts or to be the offspring of a horrible relationship. The fact is that God has a plan for them beyond the circumstances of their birth and upbringing."

With each foster child, Peter asks God, *What have You placed in this child? What talents, gifts, and potential can I tap into?* And God has responded many times by revealing their gifts and His plan for letting them flourish. "We have seen their hidden blessings come to life, and that is part of the reward for being a foster parent," Peter said.

AN IMPORTANT MISSION

Peter and Isabel have been called to serve as foster parents because they are such a great team. They both have full-time jobs, but Isabel's boss allows her to work from home most of the time, and they have a big support team of friends and family members. Theirs is a very difficult yet rewarding and important ministry.

In Mark 10:13–16, Jesus stopped His disciples from turning away parents who were bringing their children to him so that He might touch them. He told his followers: "Let the children come to me; do not hinder them, for to such belongs the kingdom of God" (verse 14).

Not everyone is called to be a foster parent, but watching Peter and Isabel, I have seen the glory of God revealed. They are bringing children to Him to be touched by faith. The fruit of their sacrifice and labor is inspiring. Their mission of evangelism is one of the most important I can think of.

CHANGING LIVES FOR THE BETTER

My friend Michael Reagan is another proponent of foster parenting and adoption. He was adopted himself as an infant by two famous actors who had just married: Jane Wyman and Ronald Reagan (yes, the future president of the United States). Michael's adoptive parents divorced when he was just three years old, and he spent most of his childhood in boarding schools and summer camps. His was not a happy childhood despite his parents' wealth and fame.

At age seven he was sexually abused by a camp counselor, which resulted in many years of shame and emotional and behavioral problems. Fortunately, he eventually married a Christian woman who helped him give his life to Jesus Christ after years of struggling. He became a radio talk-show host and Christian speaker as well as an advocate for poor, neglected, and abused children.

The Michael Reagan Center for Advocacy and Research has partnered since 2005 with Arrow Child and Family Ministries, a Christian group that works on behalf of needy children and families. As part of their efforts, the Reagan Center and Arrow Ministries encourage Christian churches to recruit foster and adoptive parents from their congregations. Michael said there are hundreds of thousands of Christian churches in the United States, and if they joined the program in great numbers, it would eventually eliminate or greatly relieve the need for foster parents and group homes.

Michael noted that the apostle James calls upon churches to do this:

> Religion that is pure and undefiled before God the Father is this: to visit orphans and widows in their affliction, and to keep oneself unstained from the world. (James 1:27)

Personally, I love this idea! I'm all for churches of all denominations and nondenominations coming together, putting their differences aside, and putting faith into action. Arrow Ministries takes its name from the Bible passages that tell us children are a gift from God and "like arrows in the hand of a warrior." They must be guided skillfully and given direction to follow God's aim for them.

Michael and Arrow Ministries also share my concern for children who are victimized by human traffickers. In my travels around the world, I've witnessed firsthand the horrors and abuses inflicted on children of all ages who are torn from their families and enslaved. I've seen them forced to labor in mines, fields, and sweatshops. Others are kidnapped by militants who threaten to kill them if they don't serve in their armies. Still others are forced to serve as sex slaves around the world.

I once spoke to 650 teenage girls who had been freed from sex slavery at a brothel in Mumbai, India. Some of them had babies in their arms. Most felt they had no reason to hope for better lives for themselves or their children. They had nowhere to go, no guidance on how they might create better lives, and no God to pray to for strength. Yet I've seen former sex slaves accept help and find redemption and healing by giving their lives to Jesus.

I've observed the miracle of these saved young Christian women who—although they were enslaved and horribly mistreated—go back to the pimps and madams who beat them up and abused them and tell them, "I love you because Jesus loves you, and I forgive you because Jesus forgave me." They have completely changed the course of their lives when shown compassion and given guidance.

As someone born with major disabilities, I'm well aware that I easily could have ended up in the foster system or an orphanage where predators might have made my life miserable. Those of us born into loving Christian families should take every opportunity to share and extend our blessings to the less fortunate among us, especially God's children.

I can't think of a better way to serve our Lord than to rescue these innocents, mend their hearts and minds, show them unconditional love, and teach them to follow Jesus Christ. Arrow Ministries helps churches create their own programs for foster and adoptive parents, showing them how to recruit, train, support, and provide resources for those who step up to save this and future generations.

PROVIDING REFUGE

I also support the work of the creators of another innovative outreach for young people rescued from sex trafficking. Hope Refuge was founded by a former missionary couple, Bob and Michelle Ryan, who operated a Christian retreat camp for foster kids and at-risk youths in California for many years.

In 2013, they joined with longtime friends and fellow missionaries, Sally and Chuck Cook, to provide a caring and supportive retreat where trafficking survivors can heal from the trauma of abuse, abandonment, and neglect. There are nearly three hundred thousand American young people put at risk by sex-trafficking criminal enterprises each year, but there are all too few safe places for those rescued from such operations to heal and recover from what is often substantial physical, mental, and emotional trauma, according to the Cooks.

Hope Refuge was created to be just such a place. It sits on 214 acres of serene woods and hills overlooking the Pacific Ocean near Santa Barbara, California. The founders describe it as a perfect natural environment for those who have suffered to find rest and healing and to begin preparing for a better future.

"Our hope is to see them empowered to think forward toward a future where their dreams and unique potential can be personally realized and shared with others," said Bob Ryan.

His team seeks to provide a caring presence in the lives of young people who have come from cruel and uncaring backgrounds. Hope Refuge offers weekend and weeklong retreats that are like first-class spa visits, with meals cooked by a professional chef and beautifully furnished rooms. To help the former sex trafficking victims relax, there are activities including trips to the beach, swimming, pool parties, surfing lessons, zip-line and high-ropes outings, Pilates classes, and barbecues. Therapeutic programs include planting trees on the site of a brush fire. There are also quiet times when the visitors can just reflect and rest so they can begin to heal and move forward.

Opening the door to faith and building trust are goals of the retreat. Its founders want to help the abused young people become aware of the power and love of God so they can transform their lives and move into a new season.

Many of the young people feel abandoned and unworthy of love. They've known only cruelty and abuse, so they are wary of trusting anyone. This is their opportunity to begin trusting again and to start looking for a greater purpose for their lives.

The Hope Refuge founders work with Saving Innocence, which rescues children from sex trafficking operations in the Los Angeles area, as well as with law enforcement and other organizations that combat human trafficking in the region.

DARE TO DREAM BIG

I am always encouraging Christians to dream big in their outreach efforts. Some get it. Others don't. Tommy and Matthew Barnett not only get what it means to dream big but may be among the biggest Christian dreamers I've ever met.

Check that. They aren't just big dreamers, they are big doers. How many other people have purchased an abandoned hospital campus, rehabbed it, and transformed it into an incredible community resource for those who need God's love?

Although I've known and admired them for years, I recently reconnected with this father-and-son team, and I am in awe of what they've accomplished. They inspire me, and I hope they inspire many others to put their Christian faith into action on such a grand scale.

Back in 1994, Tommy and Matthew founded the Los Angeles Dream Center as a home missions project. Their church was averaging just forty-eight people each Sunday when they began, now their ministry reaches more than fifty thousand per month.

Their Dream Center is the former Queen of Angels Hospital in the bleak inner core of Los Angeles. It's just nine and a half miles west of Beverly Hills but totally removed from its glitz and glamour. Their mission is rescuing and rehabilitating those suffering from addictions, homelessness, and abuse, including victims of human trafficking.

Tommy was a senior pastor at Arizona's Phoenix First Assembly of God. In 1996 his son Matthew, then in his twenties, began pastoring a small home missions church for the homeless and destitute in some of the most dangerous neighborhoods in Los Angeles.

Seven years earlier, the Queen of Angels Hospital, which served the poorest residents of the city, had been shut down and mostly vacated. The shuttered medical center, founded in 1926, was once the largest teaching hospital west of the Mississippi. It had grown to include nine buildings on eight acres in LA's despairing Echo Park neighborhood.

When it closed, the entire property was put on the market for $10 million. The owner turned down several offers from Hollywood entertainment groups before selling it to the Barnetts for $3.9 million because of their vision to transform it into a spiritual healing center. Today, the property is home to the "church that never sleeps" and a dedicated staff.

The Barnetts raised funds and used government grants to transform the decrepit hospital and its campus. They initially spent about a million dollars per floor to renovate the fifteen-floor main building and bring it up to code. Now those floors serve the destitute, troubled, and victimized. They invested $25 million more in transforming nine floors into housing for the homeless. A government tax credit grant of nearly $50 million (worth about $15 million) helped them complete renovations to the rest of the Dream Center. They say the Dream Center has more than 250 ministries, which along with housing include programs for drug addiction, unwed mothers, and AIDS victims among others.

They are truly doing God's work and following the path of Jesus on earth. The Dream Center is a place of hope and opportunity and a ripe field for harvesting new Christians. Tommy and Matthew Barnett believe in finding needs and filling them, finding hurts and healing them. In the process, they bring souls to Christ.

I spoke at their church and always enjoy visiting them and seeing how they serve others in such amazing ways. They transform lives with the power of God's love. They are meeting people where they are, serving those with desperate needs, and showing the world the power of our Christian faith.

EXTREME EMPOWERMENT

As the Barnetts have demonstrated, Christian outreach can come in many forms. It doesn't have to be packaged in the usual box. Some of the most effective programs I've seen are the most creative—and in one case extreme!

My friends Bryan and Mindy Schwarz founded Xtreme Mobility Camps Inc. (XMO) in 2008 after spending nearly thirty years as volunteer camp directors with National Camps for the Blind of Christian Record Services. Their XMO Camps provide blind and visually impaired youth with opportunities for extreme action sports, empowering them to push themselves physically and mentally to venture beyond any limitations and create more engaging and fulfilling lives.

They offer visually impaired guests a winter camping program that can include snow skiing, snowboarding, cross-country skiing, driving a snowmobile, sledding on tubes, and sleigh rides. They also put on summer camps in Colorado and California that offer surfing, wakeboarding, water-skiing, tubing, Jet Skiing, and mountain hiking.

All their camp events are centered in a Christian atmosphere, yet being Christian is not a requirement for those who attend. The Schwarz family said they have seen God's miraculous powers change the lives of their campers, whether it was freeing someone from drug abuse or alcoholism or demon possession. They have found their campers and staff, too, are more open to the Word of God when they are fully engaged physically and mentally in nature's most beautiful settings.

The Schwarz family members say their camps are tools for sharing faith and demonstrating Christian principles and beliefs. They don't push participants but instead allow them to observe and enjoy God's earthly blessings in the form of gorgeous scenery, camaraderie, and caring companionship.

Bryan and Mindy share their testimony on the final day of each camp, and the responses are often very moving. As Mindy said on their website, "We have watched Jesus melt the hardest hearts and witnessed many give their lives to Christ."*

BIBLE STUDY ON THE NATIONAL MALL

The Schwarz family helps campers enjoy God's creation in nature. Another family I've come to know, the Greens, are creating an incredible place to explore God's Word in the US capital. I've been friends for several years

* See www.xmocamps.org.

now with the Greens, a Christian family from Oklahoma City, who have many hobbies. Make that many Hobby Lobby *stores.*

Way back in 1970 David and Barbara Green borrowed six hundred dollars to start a home-based business making miniature picture frames. They opened a small store two years later, and today their retail arts and crafts business has seven hundred stores in forty-seven states with thirty-two thousand employees.

As they've built their $3.7 billion business empire, which also includes the Mardel book store chain and Hemispheres furniture stores, the Greens and their children—Matt, Steve, and Darsee—have become major fosterers of faith. They have provided hundreds of millions of dollars in support to evangelical Christian programs and outreaches, including my own. Recently they asked me to play a small role in what will likely prove to be their most remarkable and lasting contribution to Christian evangelism and to all believers.

In November 2017 they will open to the public their privately funded Museum of the Bible near the National Mall in Washington DC. This is truly a museum of biblical proportions. It will be eight stories tall with exhibits spread over 430,000 square feet. The Greens will display more than forty thousand artifacts, including ancient biblical manuscripts, Torah scrolls, some Dead Sea scrolls, and cuneiform texts from their private collection, the largest in the world. The exhibits will also include artwork, ancient ritual pieces, and, for pop music fans of Elvis Presley, his personal Bible.*

I was honored when the Greens asked me to participate in the creation of an exhibit that features interviews with Christians who talk about how reading the Bible impacted their lives. I won't have to quit my day job or move to Washington DC to appear every day that the museum is open because, like the other interview subjects, I'll appear as a hologram. How

* See www.museumofthebible.org and www.hobbylobby.com/about-us/our-story.

cool is that! I mean, I've always been very transparent, but now you will be able to see right through me!

The Museum of the Bible is led by Steve Green, who told me his vision is to create a place that tells the story of the Bible and its history over hundreds of years. The museum will welcome people of all faiths, believers and nonbelievers, in its goal "to bring to life the living Word of God, to tell its compelling story of preservation, and to inspire confidence in the absolute authority and reliability of the Bible."

Steve and his family believe the more we study and learn about the Bible, the stronger our faith will be. They want their collection to serve also as a beacon to draw and inspire nonbelievers and people of other faiths so they, too, might bask in the beauty of God's Word and even be transformed by it.

THE FRIENDS AND FAMILY PLAN

I love that so many people around the world are finding creative and unusual ways to share their faith and grow God's army. Church leaders, too, including my friends at LifeChurch in Coppell, Texas, are doing outreach in new and interesting ways.

My wife, Kanae, was living with her mother, sister, and brother in suburban Dallas when we first met. They attended LifeChurch, which is just north of Dallas/Fort Worth International Airport. Whenever I was in Dallas, Kanae and I would attend her family's church, and I got to know senior pastors Tim and Abigail Holland. Tim tells people that the first time he saw me sitting in his congregation he nearly forgot his sermon. He'd seen my videos on YouTube, and he'd even caught my appearance on *Oprah,* so it threw him off to find me in his congregation.

Tim completed his wonderful sermon. We talked afterward, and Kanae and I have been friends with Abigail and Tim ever since. Tim may be a pastor, but he is the son of missionaries, and that is really what he is at heart. In 1991, his parents, Rafael and Donna Holland, founded the Hispanic sister church of LifeChurch, Iglesia Mundo de Fe ("World of Faith Church"), in Coppell, and they now serve as spiritual leaders of that church and several others they've planted in Latin America and Spain.

It's not surprising, then, that Christian outreach is one of the fundamental values of LifeChurch. The Hollands, their church leadership team, and the church members are very active in the community. They work with a mobile soup kitchen organization to feed the hungry. Another team visits nursing homes, and yet another group brings hot coffee and breakfast treats to day laborers waiting to be picked up for jobs around the city.

The Hollands are very creative in sharing their faith and bringing more souls to God's light. I joined them at a weeklong outreach in early 2016 that was especially interesting. They encouraged fourteen hundred church members to invite at least ten friends, family members, neighbors, or complete strangers to hear me speak as part of the campaign.

What was even more impressive was that six months before they invited anyone, the congregation committed to daily prayer for each person who would be invited. They asked God to prepare their hearts to receive the invitation well.

As I watched from backstage before my speech, I had a sense of what it must have felt like to watch Jesus multiply the five loaves of bread and two fish to feed five thousand who had followed Him to a remote village. The difference was that the Hollands and their congregation multiplied the fourteen hundred church members into fourteen thousand in the audience! Even better, we had more than fourteen hundred people answer the altar call for six straight nights and give their lives to Jesus Christ.

I think of this type of outreach as the Friends and Family Plan, but it can include coworkers, neighbors, and, yes, strangers who are interested in learning about your church and your faith. The most impressive part of this outreach was that the church followed up with each individual and family to help them get plugged into the local church as members. Out of

1,414 decision cards filled out (sometimes with one card representing entire families), 20 percent of them called LifeChurch / Mundo de Fe their home church. They attend each week to grow in their personal walk with Jesus. A 20-percent increase in membership in one week is a very good week. Are you kidding? That was awesome.

FOSTERING FAITH

In this chapter, I've offered several examples of out-of-the-box and creative ways in which Christians are sharing their faith. I know there are many Christians who have jobs and families and other responsibilities that don't allow them to work full time at sharing their faith, so I wanted to wrap up this chapter by giving you a few simpler but proven ways everyone can do Christian outreach by serving as God's ambassadors.

We can help share the reality of His love and encourage others to experience it by answering their questions, welcoming their interest, offering witness, showing them how caring and compassionate Christians can be, teaching them God's Word, and living according to God's commandments.

I encourage everyone to do what they can to reach out. The most basic methods available to all Christians include:

- going to church
- inviting nonbelievers to a church service, Bible study, and Christian youth group
- welcoming visitors to your Christian services and events, taking the time to answer questions or serve their needs
- giving helpful gifts to guide visitors, including Bibles, devotionals, Christian books, and prayer guides

Part II

Building the Team

6

BLESSED ARE THE MENTORS

Jesus came down to our world to atone for our sins. The Son of God also was sent "to save the lost." He was the first and the ultimate spiritual mentor on earth, and it is a duty and a great blessing for every Christian who is secure in faith to serve as a role model and, if possible, become a mentor for those still in need of a path to eternal salvation.

God's Son ensured that His work would continue by serving as the mentor for His twelve apostles. As we are told in Luke 9:1–2, Jesus "called the twelve together and gave them power and authority over all demons and to cure diseases, and he sent them out to proclaim the kingdom of God and to heal." He also gave them detailed instructions on how to do that, even telling them what not to pack for the road when they traveled to preach the gospel: "No staff, nor bag, nor bread, nor money; and do not have two tunics" (verse 3).

Now that is some serious mentoring advice! Jesus set the example with His disciples who multiplied His work and spread His teachings after His death, resurrection, and ascension. They also encouraged others to be mentors. In the Bible, Peter says we should be "examples to the flock."

I believe all Christians have a duty to serve as guides and encouragers to others, nonbelievers and believers. They should step into that role once they are in a personal relationship with Jesus Christ and have reached a point where they have valuable experiences and expertise to share. In my case, the timing snuck up on me. I had never thought of myself as a role model or mentor until younger people began coming to me for advice and guidance.

I was busy building and pursuing my career during my teens and through my twenties. I considered myself more a student than a teacher during that period of my life. Yet as I matured in faith and developed my purpose, mentoring came naturally to me when I was approached by younger people who wanted to become public speakers, ministers, missionaries, or evangelists. I realized in my thirties that I was mentoring people without knowing it and that I actually had enough experiences and accumulated wisdom to help others.

I wouldn't feel worthy of that role without God's help and the Holy Spirit's guiding. My role as a spiritual mentor is modeled on that of the apostle Paul, who said in 1 Corinthians 11:1, "Follow my example, as I follow the example of Christ" (NIV). Mentoring isn't always easy, even with help from the Holy Spirit, because I am a mere human and therefore not perfect, neither as a man nor as a Christian. I can only try to be the best I can and hope I keep growing in faith and improving in God's eyes, and that is all I ask of those who seek guidance.

Proverbs 9:9 sums it up nicely: "Give instruction to a wise man, and he will be still wiser; teach a righteous man, and he will increase in learning."

BLESSED ARE THE HUMBLE WHO MENTOR

I enjoy mentoring as a way of guiding those younger than I around the mistakes I made at their age. I always feel refreshed and uplifted when I see them learn and apply the lessons to be better Christians. It's as if I've given them a gift that will make their journey smoother. God created us as a family, so I see anyone I mentor as a younger sibling I want to help. That is the beauty of having a family of God. We look out for each other.

Christian philosopher C. S. Lewis had another way of looking at the mentoring role: "Think of me as a fellow-patient in the same hospital who, having been admitted a little earlier, could give some advice."* I like that humble approach. Humility is an essential part of being a mentor. If you present yourself as infallible and all-knowing, what could anyone hope to learn from you?

The mentor who claims to have never made a mistake isn't a mentor anyone should want to follow. I look for mentors who have taken risks, stumbled now and then, and learned lessons in the process, because I believe they can help me avoid making the mistakes they made. I've always been up front about my flops and failures, and the lessons I've taken away from them make me a better mentor.

I have trusted the wrong people, made impetuous decisions, and tried to do too much in too little time. I've sometimes stretched myself so thin I was afraid of snapping like a rubber band. Some of those mistakes cost me money, friendships, and substantial effort. A few were downright painful, but I learned from them, and they have made me a better mentor for those who now come to me for advice, guidance, and support.

Mentoring is not the easiest thing to do. It takes time and serious thought, because you don't want to steer someone down the wrong path or give them out-of-date or just bad information. It's easier to give by writing a check as a donation or volunteering at a soup kitchen, certainly. Taking someone under your wing and serving as a confidante and spiritual guide for an extended period is much more challenging and time consuming. Sometimes when I suggest mentoring to other Christians, they say they aren't qualified or strong enough in faith, but anyone who has experienced a long journey of faith can impart godly wisdom, encouragement, and support.

* C. S. Lewis, "A Letter to Sheldon Vanauken" (April 22, 1953), in Sheldon Vanauken, *A Severe Mercy* (San Francisco: HarperSanFrancisco, 1987), 134.

Mentoring can be as simple as having a cup of coffee with someone every week or two and sharing thoughts on how to follow a godly life. Or it can be as in-depth as working side by side on a project. I'm always glad to help those who may not be as mature in their faith and walk with Jesus Christ. I want to help them be accountable and to grow and be happy in the Lord.

CARRYING ON THE WORK OF THE APOSTLES

Many churches have formal mentoring programs in which experienced Christians guide younger church members, those who have just been saved or those who are exploring their spiritual options. My Christian mentoring relationships have been informal arrangements that sprang out of friendships with young people who asked for my assistance after hearing me speak or reading my books.

While I'm sure most of them have been brought to me by God, sometimes His role is more obvious than others. This was particularly true in the case of my friend Bradon Schwarz, who considered me a role model for several years before we had even met.

Bradon was reared by Bryan and Mindy, who have a construction business in California and operate the Xtreme Mobility Camps in Colorado and California. Bradon rebelled against his parents and their faith during much of his childhood. "People were always talking to me about God and His plan for me, but I didn't care about religion. I did just about anything I could to get in trouble for some reason," he recalled.

He was twelve years old when his parents talked him into attending a Christian youth rock-concert weekend. Bradon was still not interested in faith, and he was not a fan of Christian music, but he'd never been to a concert, so he agreed to go. Since he had been homeschooled, Bradon saw this as a rare chance to hang out with other kids. He discovered that he liked the wilder Christian bands, especially Family Force 5, the Atlanta band known for its hard partying and mosh-pit blend of music styles, including rap, metal, and techno-pop.

OPENING ACT

On the final night of the concert weekend in 2007, Bradon went to hear Family Force 5 perform. He arrived early and discovered their warm-up act was a strange dude with no limbs: me!

"Nick started out cracking jokes and playing on a drum set, so I thought he was a comedian opening for the band," Bradon said. "Then he began talking about the Lord, and I felt he was talking directly to me. Nick broke down the walls I'd put up about my parents' faith. He used humor and his testimony about God's plan for his life. Back then he was like me, a young single guy, so it was different hearing it from him. When he said, 'God has a plan for you,' it stayed with me."

Bradon and I did not meet that day, but shortly after that he gave his life to Christ. His parents were thrilled, and he remembers that first time he heard me speak as a "huge event" in his life. I have no doubt God brought us together that night at the Christian concert, but apparently He was not done with us.

Fast-forward six years. By that time, I'd married Kanae, and she was a few months' pregnant with our first child. One day we went shopping because Kanae wanted some flip-flops. We walked into a store at a mall near our home in California. I saw a young sales guy standing at the back of the store and folding clothes for the display, and something about him struck me. I thought he looked like a young man who had a bright future doing bigger things.

I went to him and asked him if he could help us. Bradon eagerly introduced himself and said he recognized me from the Christian concert six years earlier! He told me the whole story about how my speech that night had helped bring him to Christ and changed his life dramatically. If I'd had any doubts God was at work, they were dispelled when Bradon revealed he'd just started working at that store that very same day! He'd walked in a week or so earlier, and they'd offered him a position on the spot. That's crazy, isn't it? Who knew God was a recruiter for clothing stores! Of course, He isn't, but God did seem to be working pretty hard at putting me in a position to mentor Bradon. So let me tell you how it all unfolded in a rather interesting manner.

After we found the flip-flops, I asked Bradon if I could pray for him and his continued walk with Jesus. He said that would be terrific. Now, once again, we parted without exchanging e-mail addresses or phone numbers. That could well have been the end of any contact between us.

Yet once again, God was not done with us! About three weeks later, Kanae and I went to a nursery to find some trees for our yard. We were looking around when a man approached us. He said his son was a big fan who'd given his life to God after seeing me speak at a concert. I realized he was Bradon's father, just as he was telling me that his son had waited on us. The connections struck me as even more remarkable when Bryan Schwarz said he knew my uncle Batta and his family, because my cousin Lara had performed at a fund-raiser for a nonprofit run by the Schwarz family.

After we spoke a bit more, Bryan offered to put the palm trees we'd bought into his truck and deliver them to our house. When he came by with the trees, he explained he was a building contractor and offered to help with any construction projects we might need. We were doing some remodeling, and he ended up helping with it.

One day while Bryan was working at our house, he gave me a video, saying it was about the nonprofit he'd started. I told him I'd had a bunch of calls and couldn't watch it right away. But I gave him one of *my* videos, which he thought was pretty funny since I didn't have time to watch his! We both laughed at that.

Later when I watched his video, I was impressed. Bryan and his wife, Mindy, had founded Xtreme Mobility Camps more than twenty years earlier. As I mentioned earlier, their camps provide sporting experiences to visually impaired campers at their vacation home in Colorado and at locations in California.

Clearly God brought Bradon and his parents and his sister, Marleigh, into our lives. Soon Kanae and I were visiting them in Colorado. We became good friends with the entire family. At one get-together, Bradon told me he'd enrolled in a Christian college and would be majoring in business because he planned on taking over and expanding Xtreme Mobility Camps one day. I offered to mentor him based on my experiences with my own nonprofit, Life Without Limbs.

When Kanae and I first visited them in Colorado for a week, I really got to know Bradon better. One night he was reading his Bible, and I offered to have devotions with him. Bradon was overwhelmed at my offer because, he reminded me, I'd helped him find his path to Jesus years before at the concert.

That night we shared our walks with Christ. Bradon had questions and asked my advice about how to stay in faith despite the temptations of daily life. We had many such discussions that week because I brought along a special wheelchair with treads that enabled me to hike in the mountains and woods alongside Kanae and Bradon. We bonded even more on those walks.

I shared my experiences traveling around the world, including some of the miracles I had witnessed. I told Bradon I'd often prayed for a miracle that would give me arms and legs. We talked in depth about why God might give some people miracles but not others. We agreed that often we cannot understand God's ways because our vision is limited, so we have to take on faith that He is working in our best interests.

BUILDING BONDS

Over the next year or so, Kanae and I became good friends with Bradon and his family. I offered them guidance on their nonprofit and on creating a board of advisors for it. I also spoke at their annual fund-raiser, which drew five thousand people. Bradon was in charge of the event, his first major fund-raiser. I offered guidance to help him put it together and, later, offered suggestions to help his family put together a business plan for their camps.

When Bradon turned twenty, he was in his second year of business school and looking ahead to running his family's camps. He was also considering whether to take business internships. I told him I was planning a series of trips around the world and needed to hire another caregiver to assist me during those travels. I offered Bradon the position, explaining I would mentor him on nonprofits and on matters of faith during our travels together.

My traveling would take just ten days a month out of his schedule. Because I had two other rotating caregivers, Bradon would be able to do other things. He prayed on my offer for a couple of days before accepting it.

SERVING GOD'S PURPOSE

I began this story by saying this long-term mentorship grew naturally out of a friendship. This is true to an extent, but you can see the hand of God at work. I believe this is true of most Christian mentoring relationships. Our heavenly Father runs the most powerful mentoring program of all!

He is the invisible hand. He brought me together with Bradon first at the concert and then at his store; then He sent Bradon's father to the nursery to bring us all together.

"Nick introduced me to Christ, and he has mentored me to help me mature in faith. God brought us together for His reasons," Bradon said. "I see so much of Nick's heart through his actions. He has such a heart for God and His ministry. He's shown me that the role of an evangelist is more than just preaching. He takes it into his relationships and helps everyone around him become closer to the person God wants them to be."

7

SERVING AS A CHRISTIAN ROLE MODEL

I can't always serve as a mentor to those I want to help, but I do my best to answer any questions they have and to be a Christian role model for them. Ideally, I could mentor anyone and everyone who seeks spiritual guidance and assistance from me. In most cases, however, I can't always be available due to my travels and other duties as the head of Life Without Limbs and Attitude Is Altitude, not to mention my role as a husband and the father of two sons.

I can serve far more people as a role model with the help of social media, such as Facebook and Twitter, which allows me to send out regular messages of hope and inspiration to those who follow me online. Mentoring is usually done one on one and in person, which requires more time and effort, not to mention easy access on a regular basis.

Organizations like Big Brothers Big Sisters of America and church youth groups can pair mentors and mentees. You can also sometimes mentor more than one person at a time if they are easily accessible.

Unfortunately, I travel so much and have so many other responsibilities that I rarely get to mentor anyone on a daily, one-on-one basis. Bradon is a rare exception, but he was working with me as a caregiver for an extended period, so that provided ample opportunities for my mentoring.

The next best thing you can do as a Christian to help others in their journey of faith is to be a role model, a good example and inspiration to others from afar. I started as a role model with Bradon and then moved into the mentor role when he came to work with me. More often I serve as a role model who occasionally meets with followers or sometimes never meets them in person. This can still be a rewarding and enlightening experience for both of us, as exemplified by Khaavion Stone, a young man I met during a visit to Nashville.

Having goals is always important, and so is taking steps toward them. The results are up to God. Each person must acquire knowledge and grow in faith. Christian mentors share, encourage, and strengthen by the grace of God. Do not be discouraged if circumstances change. Those seeking to grow will have changing needs, priorities, and opinions as they mature in faith. Mentors can't control everything. They serve as guides and encouragers, and whenever possible, try to keep people on the correct path God wants them to follow. Not all seasons of intentional mentoring end up the way we think, but as God calls us to, we serve to see more of His children spurred on to complete His will.

ROLE MODELING UNDER GOD'S GUIDANCE

Shynithia Stone was four months pregnant when her doctor gave her life-changing news: the baby she was carrying had not developed arms and legs. The doctor, who had never delivered an infant without limbs, tried to persuade Shynithia, who was only twenty-one years old and single, to abort the baby right away. She broke down in tears.

This caring mother offers her story here, and I think it is a beautiful testimony to the power of a mother's love and God's love, too:

> I was so excited when I found out that I was expecting. I couldn't wait to get my first ultrasound and see a picture of my baby. When I did, I couldn't quite understand what the doctors were showing me or what they were telling me about my son. Yes, the ultrasound pictures clearly showed us that our baby was a boy. All I could hear and process was the doctors telling me that this child would not have a meaningful life, that this child would not be able to do anything for himself, that I would have to do everything for him, that basically I would eventually get tired of doing everything for him, and that most likely he would wind up being put into an institution, which would not be fair to him or to me.
>
> In short, the doctors told me that the best thing for this child I was carrying, and the best thing for me, was to get an abortion as soon as possible. My cousin LaMonica McDonald went with me to the ultrasound appointment, and we both just cried. I had to get out of the doctor's office and get to my mother so she could explain this to me in terms I could understand.
>
> I showed my mother the pictures, and she told me that my baby's arms and legs had not developed. She told me also that the hospital had called her and repeatedly told her the same things they told me about getting an abortion as the best option. They told her to try to convince me that this would be better for me in the long run. They said that I was very young and I could have other children. But they didn't know any of the history of my family or our religious beliefs and where we came from.
>
> You see, we are of the Apostolic Faith, Baptized in the Name of Jesus, Holy Ghost Spirited, Speaking in Tongues, God Fearing Saints that believe in the Doctrine of My Lord and Savior Jesus Christ.

There is nothing too hard for God. I remember all of the teachings I learned as a child in Sunday school, and I started praying to God to show me the way. *Let my thoughts be His thoughts.* And He did.

I picked out my son's name, which is Khaavion Auriiz Stone. I had a baby shower and did all the normal things a new mother does when expecting. After the experience with the doctors at the hospital, the only ones that knew about Khaavion's not having any limbs were my mother and my cousin. My mother and I did not want anyone else trying to interfere in God's plans for my baby and my life, so we left Khaavion's fate in God's grace.

When the doctors said the hospital recognized that abortion was not in God's plans for me and my son, opportunities started opening up for us. They connected me with the special nurses and at-home care. You see, Khaavion has always had angels in his corner. His fourth angel was a public health nurse who worked in the department of nurses for newborns. Her name was Nancy. She fought for Khaavion as though he were her very own son. Nancy opened up many lines of communication with different doctors and organizations that would best benefit my son.

When the doctors at Vanderbilt Hospital said they could not do something, Nancy said, "Yes you can, and you will." Nancy helped me get prosthetic arms made for Khaavion. Nancy went to all the doctor appointments so she could explain all the medical terms the doctors used when talking about my son. Nancy helped get Khaavion enrolled into Tennessee Early Intervention Services (TEIS), which provided me with a specialist who could help me develop and encourage Khaavion's physical skills. They also provided Khaavion with other agencies that would help, including the Arc of Davidson County, Tennessee, plus the Shriners here in Nashville and the Shriners Hospital of Lexington, Kentucky.

Nancy also helped get him enrolled in the outpatient pediatric physical therapy program at Vanderbilt. When he outgrew that program, she helped me get him into the Susan Gray School at Vanderbilt University Hospital. Then he entered the program at Harris-Hillman, and that is where he met his fifth angel, Sally. You see, when you come from a God-fearing, blessed, and saved family, God will surround you with an unlimited number of earthly angels.

I am Khaavion's first angel as his mother. My mother, Linda Stone, is his second. His third is my fiancé, Phillip Deark, the only true father he knows and loves. His fifth angel is Sally, who has opened doors for my son with her caring and loving personality. Sally is a very special person, who didn't stop until she made it possible for Khaavion to meet Nick.

My entire family and I are so grateful and honored that Nick decided to add Khaavion's story, my son's own first chapter, to this book. There will be many more chapters to come from Khaavion's beautiful life. You see, Khaavion is eight years old now and thriving with love and abundance through the grace of God. My entire family loves Sally for her genuine love for Khaavion. Sally is and will always be a member of our family through the blood of Jesus Christ.

Shynithia's story is quite moving to me, of course. My own parents had no warning I would be born without limbs, even though my mother had received all the usual tests and sonograms. In her case, Shynithia had some time to prepare for the birth of her son and, unlike my parents, she had the Internet to help her search for answers her doctors could not provide. I am grateful her online research led her to my videos and websites, because it allowed me to serve as a role model and a source of hope for her and, later, her son, Khaavion.

"When I started researching to see if there were other people born without limbs, Nick popped up right away. Then a friend at my church gave me one of his books. I had always planned on raising my son, but it helped to know that Nick had found God's purpose for him. It gave me hope that my son would find his purpose too," she says.

When Shynithia's doctor and others kept pressing her to have an abortion because they didn't think her son could have a normal life, she showed them my videos as proof that, with a loving and supportive family, strong faith, and determination, a child without limbs could have a ridiculously good life. "My pregnancy was great, except whenever I went to my doctor, they kept saying this baby would never be able to do anything. I had seen Nick's videos and all that he had done," Shynithia says. "When I showed them to my doctor, he was surprised. He had never seen anyone like Nick. Then he warmed up to the possibilities for my child, too."

A ROLE TO BE WELCOMED

I share Shynithia and Khaavion's story with you because my relationship with them is similar to relationships I have with many others around the world. In my travels I've met at least thirty people born without arms and legs. I am grateful to know them and to offer them hope and assistance because I believe that is one of my God-given purposes in this life.

Shynithia and Khaavion are among the many people who first found me through social media and the Internet. They followed me and allowed me to be Khaavion's role model, and then, like many others, they found an opportunity to meet me when I came to the Nashville area.

I have no doubt our meeting was part of God's plan for both of us. I give all credit to our heavenly Father, and I'm sure He would want to share a bit of it with a young lady named Sally Hamrick, who has served as Khaavion's tutor, advocate, and friend.

I asked her to explain how the three of us came together under God's plan. When you read her story, I'm sure you will marvel as I did at the way He brought us into each other's lives. This is another instance in which the mentor and role model benefited as much as those he sought to serve.

Be the Hands and Feet

We All Have a Purpose

By Sally Hamrick

I grew up in a family that kept me in church and taught me that trust, faith, love, and obedience to God were the most important things in life. More than that, they taught me that serving others was one of the most powerful examples of Christ we could portray on earth.

As a child, I watched my parents serve others in any way they could. They gave me a heart for others and a heart for Christ, which has provided a firm foundation in my life. After high school, I majored in early childhood education with a focus on special education at the University of Tennessee.

I worked as a missionary in Africa for a couple of years, and then I attended seminary school and worked with disabled children and their families. I went through a valley of challenging times due to the deaths of several loved ones, along with broken relationships. I was in a place of discouragement and found myself crying out to God for help and encouragement.

Amid all the chaos He calmly whispered to me that Nashville should become my home. All I could do was trust He had the best plan. I moved to Nashville and found a job as a substitute teacher in the elementary schools. Then, in 2014, I met the young man who forever changed my life. I was assigned to sub for a sweet teacher, Laura Neumann, at a wonderful school.

As she prepared me to take over her class, she ran through the students, and the last name she mentioned was Khaavion. Her face lit up as she told me about this amazing little boy who was born without limbs but managed to inspire everyone he met.

I was twenty-five years old and I'd seen quite a bit of the world, but Khaavion was the first child I'd met without arms or legs. From our first meeting, I felt God had put Khaavion in my path for a unique purpose. I was his substitute teacher, and then I became his teacher's assistant in the classroom. I knew this would be a challenge for both of us, but God instilled me with a sense of peace.

The following year was one of the most difficult and encouraging years of my life. During this time I came to know Khaavion's supportive, loving, and caring family members who have faith that he will accomplish anything he sets his mind to do.

Khaavion's new schoolmates weren't prepared for his unique appearance, and as a result, he initially had to endure many questions and, sadly, comments that were probably more hurtful than intended. Our first day in the cafeteria was met with staring and mostly silence rather than acceptance and welcoming.

Later, I learned Nick had similar experiences during his first days in the various schools he attended. Nick overcame that initial lack of acceptance in much the same way Khaavion did: by taking the initiative and charming everyone he spoke to.

I'd never seen anyone bring about such an amazing shift simply by radiating joy and hope. I observed this tiny boy make everyone around him a better person by treating them with love, kindness, and selflessness.

Khaavion transformed his kindergarten classmates from wary strangers to friends and supporters. Something about

Khaavion makes you feel accepted and loved, and that is a characteristic that not many people possess. He is truly a beautiful image of Christ in the way he loves people for who they are.

After spending about six months working with Khaavion, I began some Internet research on others born without limbs, hoping to find role models for him. He was learning to read and talk more, and I knew he was capable of a lot of things. I came across Nick, and I was amazed by what he was doing and how he was reaching out to others for the glory of God.

Every time I saw something new that Nick had conquered, it gave me more and more hope that Khaavion would be able to do some of the same things, such as swimming, moving around vertically, and operating an electric wheelchair.

At first, I did not realize that Shynithia and her mother already knew about Nick. They had been showing his videos to Khaavion to inspire him too. I love how God ordains things even before we know they are coming. He orchestrates beautiful, powerful experiences for His children in amazing ways.

As we were all watching Nick, God was watching us and ordaining a meeting between us. This would mark the first time Khaavion spoke with a man just like him, someone to give this child hope for the future.

I grew determined to give Khaavion the same inspiration he had given me. I wanted him to meet Nick and see him as a mentor who could understand him better than anyone else could. I wanted to help Khaavion see that he is not alone, that he has an essential purpose, and that, like Nick, he can do anything he sets his mind to do.

I eventually learned that Nick was scheduled to be in Nashville in July 2016. I e-mailed his office, and Nick's assistant, Karla Mills, set up a meeting for Khaavion and his family and me.

The meeting was on July 22 at Nick's hotel in Nashville. When Nick arrived, Khaavion was at first shy, which is usually how he responds to new people. By the end of their talk, however, he was smiling and being his normal lively and joyful self.

Shynithia's fiancé, who has been like a father to Khaavion since he was just fifteen months old, was there, and Nick encouraged us all in powerful ways. Others might say they have empathy for Khaavion's struggles, but Nick is one of the few who truly understands what it is like to have no limbs from birth.

Shynithia has always pushed her son to accept no limitations, and Nick supported her efforts, encouraging Khaavion to try new things and to keep striving. He spoke life into Khaavion's future.

Nick said if Khaavion wanted to go into speaking one day that he would help him, encourage him, and mentor him. He told us to consider him part of the family, and he was always available if anyone had questions.

We all prayed together at the end of the meeting, and I felt the presence of God in ways I hadn't experienced in a long time. God reminded me that He'd given each person in our circle a purpose.

As Nick prayed over the family, I smiled because I knew this was a life-changing experience for everyone present. Khaavion had someone just like him to look up to, someone to give him motivation and encouragement, to remind him that he can and will fulfill a deep purpose. For that we are all forever grateful.

Khaavion still struggles with speaking because of a speech impediment, but every time he and I look through pictures of our meeting, he says, “Nick.” He will never again feel alone because of his lack of limbs, and I will always be grateful and uplifted for Nick’s presence in his life and mine.

8

ALLIES FOR THE GOSPEL

I love the personal rewards of mentoring one on one. There is nothing quite like seeing a young person applying the advice and lessons you've imparted. I have to admit, though, that there is a lot to be said about mentoring on a much bigger scale. In some cases, I start out in a mentoring relationship, but it grows over time into a spiritual alliance in which we work toward common goals by joining forces.

That brings me to another young man I've been working with. Mentoring him may be the best of all my experiences, because I know my efforts will be multiplied many times. You see, this ambitious fellow has already been doing God's work on a large scale, recruiting hundreds of young people for His army on earth.

Brian Barcelona and his One Voice Student Missions (OVSM) are addressing concerns that, as studies have shown, fewer and fewer young people are attending church regularly. To reach this unchurched generation, Brian developed a ministry that works with local churches to go into public high schools and plant Bible clubs. Members meet at lunchtime to explore the Christian faith and open the door to those who might otherwise never find their way to our Father in heaven.

As a newspaper story on Brian's school program noted, how many other Christian missionaries know "exactly what time the non-believers will arrive, when they will break for lunch, and what time they will leave five days a week, nine months a year"?*

Brian knows how to reach young people who have doubts about their faith because he was one of them just a few years ago. Although he grew up in a Christian family—his grandfather planted five churches and was a traveling preacher—Brian watched his parents backslide in their faith and it discouraged him. He considered himself an atheist through most of his teen years.

Brian felt as though most Christians he knew did not walk the talk. He heard discussions about horrible things that occurred within the church and its members and felt Christians were hypocrites. "When I was fifteen or sixteen, I thought there was no way God could exist when those who claimed to know Him and love Him didn't live up to His teachings or commandments," he said.

One of his Christian friends invited Brian to attend his church youth group. Brian turned him down several times, but the friend kept asking him every week, refusing to give up on him. Finally, the friend threw in a special offer. He promised to buy Brian a Jamba Juice if he went to his youth group meeting. Brian, who admired his friend's persistence and the way he lived in faith, finally gave in. The Jamba Juice was a bonus.

Brian surprised himself at that meeting when he stood up in the church and dared Jesus to touch him. It was a bold move. Brian immediately felt "this crazy love come over my body." He wept.

In the months that followed, Brian accepted God's love for him. He realized it didn't matter how other Christians acted, whether they were

---

* Chelsen Vicari, "Stop Trying to 'Attract' Youth; Go to Them," *The Christian Post,* August 12, 2015, www.christianpost.com/news/stop-trying-to-attract-youth-go-to-them-142565.

hypocrites or true followers of Christ. The only thing that mattered was his personal relationship with Jesus Christ.

His own walk of faith from atheist to believer taught Brian how to reach others in their teen years, and that is what he has devoted his life to doing. He remembers that when he considered himself a nonbeliever in high school, the Christian kids walked past him every day carrying their Bibles, never stopping to even introduce themselves, let alone to share their faith. Brian admits he might have spurned any efforts to convert him or change his beliefs, but no one bothered to even try until his friend bribed him to attend his Christian youth group.

"It bothered me that they never reached out. If someone had cared enough to do that, I might have been saved sooner," Brian said. "I might not have spent so many of my formative years in high school feeling depressed and suicidal."

Once Brian accepted Jesus Christ as his Savior, he felt overwhelmed with a love more intense than any he'd ever known. For the first time in his life, he felt God was real and present in his life on a very personal level. Brian kept praying, and two years later he had a vision that God wanted to reach other high school students in the same way He'd reached him.

He started a Bible club at his alma mater, Elk Grove High School, in 2009 with about six students. Attendance grew to thirty-five and plateaued for a few months, which frustrated Brian, but he remained patient. By the end of the school year, participation had grown to more than three hundred students. Encouraged, Brian began planting Bible clubs in other schools.

In 2010 Brian dreamed of a "massive salvation" coming to a high school in Los Angeles. He moved to Southern California where he and a community of campus missionaries united and formed One Voice Student Missions. They fasted and prayed for revival in the high schools of America. The following summer, One Voice participated in an event that brought more than a thousand people, most of them students, to the Lord.

Since then, One Voice has been expanding, thanks to Brian and his team of dedicated Christian leaders. In 2016 they created seventy-six Bible clubs in just six months, with more than ten thousand students participating in the Los Angeles area. By early 2017 Brian had twenty-three volunteer staff members working full time for him. It's been incredible to see how quickly they've taken his vision to reality on a large scale. Brian has achieved this success by staying focused on his goals, or as they say in the business world, "keeping the main thing the main thing." In his case, that focus is on doing the work of Jesus on earth.

PLANTING FAITH IN SCHOOLS

A high school principal in the gang-troubled Inglewood neighborhood of Los Angeles learned just how determined my friend is when Brian visited him recently. The school was plagued with gangs and fighting. They'd just had a blowup among the students when Brian asked to meet with the principal. The skeptical principal thought his visitor was conning him at first when my friend asked, "How can we serve your school?"

The principal wasn't sure where Brian was coming from, but what first came to his mind was that a few buildings on the school grounds were in need of new paint because they were covered with graffiti. So the principal threw that out as a worthy project if Brian was looking for a way to make a contribution.

Brian agreed to return in two weeks with a paint crew and the paint. He made good on the promise. The principal then asked him, "What do you want from me and this school?" Brian said that he would like to start an extracurricular club at the school, like the chess club or lacrosse club, but this one would be for Christian students interested in studying the Bible with their peers.

The principal agreed—just as many others have.

SHARING THE GOOD NEWS

Brian believes that public high schools across the nation have deprived their students of the good news of Jesus, resulting in a generation of teens who have little or no foundation of faith. His goal is to change that by taking the gospel into the public schools. He says their approach redefines church planting for today's young people. The students experience a faith-based community during lunch hours in their schools. OVSM adopts schools and offers hope and comfort to all students, including those trying to escape drugs, alcohol, abuse, neglect, and criminal histories. Brian and his team share their beliefs, offer assistance, and let God do the rest.

The OVSM website offers the following description of Brian's ambitious faith-sharing organization:

> One Voice is more than a movement or a ministry, it's a message. This message is simple, "God is not done with the High Schools of America." Every message needs a messenger, and that is our assignment. Our community is composed of people from different nations, backgrounds, churches, and ministries. Together, we labor to reach students and campuses across America, and soon the world, with the Good News of Jesus. We have been called by God to save the lost and awaken the Church to the reality of the mission field that lies before Her. We are missionaries to students. We are missionaries to campuses. We are messengers to the nations of the world.*

This is not a pie-in-the-sky mission statement. Brian and his team have been incredibly successful in reaching students from every walk of life. Early on, he was conducting a Bible study in a school when gang members

* One Voice Student Missions, Pasadena, California, https://onevoicestudentmissions.com/what-we-do.

fleeing from school security stumbled into the room. They didn't know what else to do, so they sat down. When Brian finished the Bible study, the gang members looked at him in awkward silence before one finally stood and quietly asked, "What do I have to do to be saved?"

Later the principal of that school told Brian, "Whatever you are doing, keep doing it, because gangs have been coming to our counseling offices with kids saying, 'We don't want to be a part of our gang anymore. Help us.'"

That is exactly what One Voice was created to do. They want to help students who are trying to realize their dreams by showing them that God is the ultimate dream fulfiller. As Brian has witnessed, the Lord is also a lifesaver.

A school staff member found a note left after one of Brian's meetings. It was an anonymous letter addressed to the Bible club's president and "the guy who preached," which was me. The letter thanked us and, paraphrasing, said, "Yesterday night I was planning on killing myself, but during school I went to your meeting and I found hope and today I am alive."

Brian was deeply moved by that letter, which validated his work as a mentor on a grand scale. I have to admit, I felt pretty good about it too, as the guy mentoring the mentor!

FOLLOWING A DREAM

Brian and I share a favorite Bible passage, one that changed both our lives. When I first read the story of the blind man healed by Jesus, as told in John 9:1–4, I saw how it applied to me, and it helped me to find God's purpose for me on earth. For his part, Brian sees parallels between high school students and the blind man. Like him, many teens are born blind to God's light.

In that well-known Bible story, the disciples asked Jesus, "Rabbi, who sinned, this man or his parents, that he was born blind?" Jesus doesn't look for blame. Instead, He said, "It was not that this man sinned, or his parents, but that the works of God might be displayed in him."

That response sent me on God's path to become His recruiter of souls around the globe. It also inspired Brian to help teens find their way to Jesus Christ and everlasting life in heaven. Mentoring Brian is a gift to me. We share the same goals, and by helping him, I work with him to reach more nonbelievers and put them in God's hands.

Our heavenly Father has made it quite clear to me that mentoring others with the same mission is also part of His plan for me, because He keeps delivering young people like Brian Barcelona to me.

When we first met, Brian told me of a dream he'd had about meeting me years earlier. What follows is his description of that very interesting dream—or should we call it a premonition.

> I'm not really a dreamer, so this is really strange. I had seen Nick's videos and read about him, but this was really a random dream. I was on a golf course—another random thing—and I was with this other guy who had mentored me. Nick was there, too, even though we'd never met in real life. While we were on the course, the other mentor walked away from us, and Nick looked at me and said, "Are you ready? Let's go!" And he led me off in another direction. I followed Nick, and then I woke up.

When Brian told me about this dream and asked me what I thought of it, I had to admit it seemed to predict I would one day be a mentor for him. Brian accepted that, and I've really enjoyed working with him, because he takes what I tell him to heart and then puts it into action.

This isn't always the case with people I've mentored. Some listen but don't follow up. Brian knows I have his best interests at heart because we share the same goals, and he knows that when I challenge him, it's because I want him to succeed over the long term and on a large scale.

Brian told me that others encouraged him and told him that God was going to use him, but they left it at that. They didn't offer guidance or get involved. I have been running both a nonprofit Christian organization and a for-profit motivational business for more than a decade. I know how God can use us for His purposes if we get engaged and serve other Christians doing His work. I've had failures and successes, so I have very specific guidance to give those I mentor. I can help them avoid the mistakes I've made—but only if they are willing to act on my advice.

Brian has listened. He has learned and benefited from my experiences. Some of my mentoring advice to Brian might sound contradictory at first. For example, I've told him to think bigger while also counseling him to slow down. The early success he experienced in planting Bible clubs in inner-city high schools around LA was very exciting. Word spread among educators eager to bring positive influences into their schools. Brian received invitations to speak and start Bible clubs at schools across the country.

You might say I've helped him use his brakes more while also keeping an eye on the road ahead. Success can be as big a threat to a major outreach as failure. Brian found himself nearly overwhelmed with opportunities. I've counseled him to be disciplined, to partner with local church leaders, and to make good use of volunteer workers so he doesn't take on more than he can handle on his own.

PLANNING FOR SUCCESS

I suggested that Brian hit the pause button and take the time to create a five-year plan that built upon his initial dream and took his movement around the world. With my encouragement, Brian put together a plan to plant fifteen thousand Bible clubs across the United States. This sounds like quite a feat, I know, but Brian has a proven concept. He believes young people can be both influenced and influential. They respond to stories about God's power to change their lives. Their faith is triggered. They feel it is okay to trust and believe in the Lord.

Still, the first time I asked about his plans for One Voice, he threw out several ambitious but vague ideas. I said, "Those are great initiatives, but what is your plan?" He then restated the same vague ideas. Again I said, "But what is your plan?"

Finally, Brian shrugged his shoulders and said, "I guess I don't have a plan." We laughed at that, and then we set about creating a real plan for him and his organization. Brian had a goal of reaching twenty-six thousand high schools across the country, which was admirable. When I asked him how he planned on doing that, he said, "I don't know."

I believe in dreaming big, but my parents often told me as a young man that I needed more than a dream; I needed a plan. They were right, of course. God breathed blessings on me in my younger, innocent years. I'd dive blindly into something—like my plan to give away my entire life savings to South African orphans when I was nineteen years old—and the Lord seemed to guide me through it. Brian felt much the same way about the early days of One Voice.

When he started his first Bible club in his former high school, it took Brian about a year to get just thirty-five students to attend, but then the number of members grew swiftly. He seemed a bit dazzled by his success when we first met. God was surely working in his favor in those early days, because Brian was, without a doubt, doing His work.

Still, whether you are recruiting souls for Christ or building starter houses for first-time home buyers, early success can be both a blessing and a trap. As an organization or business grows more successful, everything gets more complicated. You need more help. You need more materials. You need more scheduling. You need more funding.

As I told Brian, you might get away without a plan at first, but eventually you will need to get organized and create a road map for long-term success. So we went to work and put together his long-term plan.

Brian, who was born in 1990, admitted that he and others of the millennial generation tend to think in the short term. He cites studies that have found millennials are often so good at expressing themselves that older people tend to assume they know more than they really do about practical things, such as organizational planning and finance. The cool thing about Brian is that he realizes this. He knows that he doesn't know. He welcomes guidance and appreciates it.

A GREATER VISION

I applaud Brian for being open to my mentoring. I encourage him and challenge him because I want him to fulfill his God-given purpose.

I tell him to pour into his team members and his students the same love, truth, and encouragement I've poured into him. I've stressed to him that one of the best investments he can make is to show his staff how much he appreciates and cares for them every day.

One Voice isn't a money-making operation. It's a life-changing operation. It doesn't have the funds to pay a huge staff, and it relies on volunteers who are true believers. Most of them are full-time volunteers, a rarity in this world, so it is important for them to know their work is valued.

Jesus attracted disciples and followers because He poured love into them. They carried on His work because of that love. Those of us who are doing His work today should follow His example.

Brian understands the true foundation of his work is in building relationships with his team members as well as with local churches, school administrators, teachers, and the students who operate and attend the Bible clubs. He has mastered the art of building relationships when he goes into schools. He doesn't immediately begin preaching the gospel or recruiting for Bible clubs. Instead, he takes time to get to know the students and teachers. And he bribes them just like his high school friend bribed him, but instead of Jamba Juice, he offers them doughnuts.

"I give away hundreds of doughnuts all over campus, and I meet with every type of student: the jocks, the gang members, the drug users. I just show them God's love and hope that they welcome me into their hearts so I can help them find a path to His kingdom. I've done this in troubled schools in LA's Compton area and in super-fancy, super-rich schools in Beverly Hills. Kids are kids and they struggle with sin everywhere, but their hearts are open if you approach them in the right manner."

SERVING WITH HUMILITY

When I speak to those I mentor about my faith, I share the good and the bad. I talk about how I came to doubt my parent's faith and the Lord during my adolescence, because I thought a loving God would not bring me into the world without limbs. I never present myself as a perfect Christian. I tell young people in particular that you can have faith and still have questions. You can have faith and make mistakes. I admit my weakness because it is the truth. I want students to relate to me, and that is something Brian picked up on by listening to me when I speak to large and small groups.

"From hearing Nick, I learned not to approach students like I think I'm the best thing to ever happen to them. Instead, I present myself as someone who can help them meet Jesus Christ, who can help them do anything through His strength and love. We welcome students of every type into our clubs whether they are gangbangers, transgenders, or homosexuals. We don't compromise our message. We tell everyone that if they are living in sin, they have to change their ways, but if they accept Jesus into their lives, the kindness of God will lead them to repentance. We tell them once you love God and have a relationship with Jesus Christ, your life will be changed forever," he said.

Young Christians teach me as much as I teach them. Brian has talked one on one with so many young people of his generation. He says it is important to understand their mind-set. They are gifted communicators, and they often seem confident and assured, but the truth is that, like all young people, they have insecurities. They may not appear to need mentoring, but once you earn their trust, they welcome it. They want someone to care enough to guide them and invest in their growth.

"This is a broad statement, but in general, I think millennials, including me, can seem very smart and confident, but we so need mentoring and discipleship. We need guidance even on basic matters, whether you are talking about building faith or building an organization. We want to build strong foundations, and we know we don't always have the knowledge and experience to do that," he said.

"I appreciate Nick because I've never before met a man so secure in his God-given path. His advice comes from a place of deep faith and security in that faith. Nick knows what God has called him to do, and he pours that into everyone he mentors and loves."

Brian says I've helped him understand there is a difference between what is good and what is God. He's grown better at discerning the good opportunities from those that are even better because they follow God's purpose for Brian's life.

"With God's help, my plan to plant Bible clubs in schools around the country is attainable, and I should pour my heart and soul into planting them," Brian said. "Nick has helped me navigate and stay on that path."

FROM MENTOR TO ALLY

Brian is only six years younger than I, and I can see our relationship evolving into more of a mutually beneficial spiritual alliance, a sort of brotherly kinship in the coming years. I have been able to help him focus on his key purpose and plan for the future, and that has been rewarding and fulfilling for me.

He is positioned to become a leader for his generation. He is wise beyond his years when it comes to understanding how to reach young people and guiding them on the path to Jesus Christ. I think we can help each other do that on an even bigger scale while glorifying God.

Brian wisely notes that when speaking to teens who are nonbelievers or searching for a spiritual home, he follows the example of the supreme Christian Mentor. Jesus used parables—for example, He compared the kingdom of heaven to a mustard seed—so people could easily grasp the basic concepts of Christian beliefs.

"Jesus spoke in ways that were real to them, and Nick does the same thing in his speeches," Brian said. "We try to follow that same model when talking to students in schools. We break down the gospel to its simplest forms. We also train our volunteers when they go into the schools to get to know students and their interests first. They need to know you care about them before they will care about what you have to say. We believe in joyful repentance that is focused on God's giving you a new and better life. It's like you give me an old dollar and I'll give you one hundred new dollars. That's a deal they will take every time. In the same manner, we show them that repentance isn't sorrowful, it is joyful."

I've learned that serving as a role model and mentor often leads to spiritual alliances with young Christian leaders who are talented and energetic and who share my passions and purpose. We are driven to bring more people to Jesus Christ. I believe that God has big plans for people like Brian Barcelona, Khaavion Stone, and Bradon Schwarz, just as He has plans for each and every one of His children who pray to Him in faith.

In the next chapter, I will tell you about one of my next projects that may include an even bigger alliance with Brian and other young Christian leaders.

9

GOD'S BIG TENT

I was preparing to speak at the Lake Avenue Church in Pasadena, California, in 2010, when someone from the church announced over the PA system that the auditorium had reached its fire-code capacity of two thousand people and no more would be admitted. Groans of disappointment could be heard across the church campus, because there were many still lined up to get in.

I remember thinking: *I've come to preach, and God is here to save, but we don't have a building big enough for all to hear.* Then I said a prayer, *God, we need a bigger venue!* As soon as those words went through my mind, a vision came to me of a huge white tent. Then a figure popped up: *eight thousand people.*

The image of a massive white tent packed with eight thousand people was still lodged in my mind when I took the stage to preach that day. I didn't mention it, but a seed had been planted. In the weeks, months, and years that followed, the vision of preaching to thousands of people in a white tent grew into a dream that I didn't know what to do with, except pray and keep it to myself for several years.

But then something stirred in me. I made a few phone calls to see if we could get a tent donated. My first four calls weren't all that helpful. My fifth call was incredible. The person said they'd just given a ministry in Africa a tent that could accommodate eight thousand people.

My emotions were mixed at that news, as you can imagine. I said to God, *Bless that ministry in Africa and thank You for confirming that even the vision of an eight-thousand-person tent was from You.* It could have been a five-thousand-person tent or any other number, but the fact that they said eight thousand was so encouraging.

I eventually shared my vision with our board of directors and asked them to join me in praying to find out if God wanted me to pursue it. I posted a note on Facebook, saying I was looking for a donated tent that size. One board member pledged a donation toward it. The idea seemed to pick up momentum.

There was just something appealingly old school—or maybe even Old Testament—about conducting worship services in a tent. I am so thankful for the support I have received from the board of Life Without Limbs over all these years. I had no concept of what our timeline would be, but when that donation pledge came through about three years ago in 2014, I told the board that it felt overwhelming to attempt something so unique, new, and big for us.

Practically speaking, in a modern world, it didn't make much sense. Big-top tents are expensive and a challenge to transport and set up, not to mention ill-suited for air-conditioning or heating when the weather is not hospitable. Why not just rent an auditorium or theater? At the same time, I was wrestling in my spirit because God's pocket has unlimited resources. The Staples Center in Los Angeles costs more than $250,000 a day to rent. I envisioned multiple nights in a row, so the tent seemed like a better option.

I had to admit this was a confusing dream, but it persisted, so I asked everyone to help me pray on it. Tents certainly are prominently mentioned in the Bible, and they've played major roles throughout the history of Christianity. The Old Testament describes the "tent of meeting" as the place where people gathered for worship. We're told in Exodus 33:8–9, "Whenever Moses went out to the tent, all the people would rise up, and each would stand at his tent door, and watch Moses until he had gone into the tent. When Moses entered the tent, the pillar of cloud would descend and stand at the entrance of the tent, and the LORD would speak with Moses."

The apostle Paul was a tent maker who used his earnings to subsidize his work as an evangelist. In more modern times, many fishers of men, including Aimee Semple McPherson, Oral Roberts, and one of my heroes, Billy Graham, traveled the country, staged tent revivals for huge audiences, and saw thousands of souls saved under the canvas roof.

Some of the people I talked to shared my enthusiasm for the throwback aspects of tents. Others said that preaching in a tent seemed like an outdated concept in our high-tech age. Why pack a few thousand people into a tent when you could reach millions on Facebook, Twitter, or YouTube?

We have explored using Livestream video feeds to expand our reach dramatically. For example, we had a Life Without Limbs event that drew 20,000 people to a rented South Florida stadium and was watched by another 144,000 online. Having our own tent as a venue appealed to me because we could control the quality of the event to a much greater degree. It would also allow us to create a more efficient and effective system for following up with those who said yes to Jesus each night. The goal is to secure long-term fruit by plugging each new person into a local church so they get the support and guidance they need to become lifetime members of the Christian community.

Some churches don't know how to create that bridge, and it's rare that an evangelist collaborates well with local churches to help guide the new members, or vice versa. Often churches and evangelists come together only for special events and don't have long-term relationships.

Evangelism is the core of what we do. We want to encourage all people in their walk with God. We want to see American churches mobilize and unify across denominations to learn how best to preach the gospel in modern times. We want to help churches relate to, reach out to, and share their own testimony with those who have not heard the good news.

The question has been what our role should be. We could offer a program to churches, or would having a large tent open up even greater potential for collaborative outreach and mutual efforts? I mulled this over for a few years. The Lord works on His own time schedule.

My attentions were diverted away from the tent concept for about five months. I hardly thought about it until I woke up one day with my brain on fire about my big-top dream. I had a day or two for brainstorming, so I fired up my laptop and did a Craigslist search for a big-venue tent. Up popped an ad in Spanish, which I now read and speak fairly well thanks to a certain wife who grew up in Mexico. It was for a tent big enough for five thousand people. The price seemed very reasonable. I called the guy who posted the ad. He sent me to the owner, who proved to be Buford Dowell, a seventy-nine-year-old former singer and evangelist who preached in tents for forty years.

In fact, he went through so many tents that he began making them as a side business. Buford was a colorful guy and a well-connected expert on tents, tent making, and big tops of every kind. Although he'd already sold the five-thousand-person tent advertised on Craigslist, he promised to keep an eye out for me.

God was at work. I could sense His presence. I had no idea how or when it would happen or even *if* it would happen, but this persistent dream was leading me somewhere. A short time later I was in Santa Barbara, California, for a speaking engagement. Afterward, I spoke with a married couple, we'll call them Caroline and Richard because they want to remain anonymous. They asked me what was going on with my mission to recruit more souls to Jesus, and I told them about my recurring dream of the big white tent. They were intrigued.

Caroline later told me that she woke up at 5 a.m. the next day and began searching for tents on the Internet. The next thing I knew, she was recruiting friends to help her in the search, including some celebrities. And momentum continued to build.

In November 2016 we made a family trip to Dallas to visit Kanae's mother and sister. Since Buford Dowell lived there too, I arranged to meet with him for the first time. He was quite a character. When we had talked on the phone, I noticed he had a very rough voice that could be difficult to understand. He explained, when we met, that during open-heart surgery a few years earlier, a nurse had ruptured his vocal cords while putting an air pipe into his esophagus. His voice was ruined.

After recounting that sad story, Buford looked at me and put it all in perspective: "But thank God for Jesus." I could see that he knew God was still at work in his life—and mine. Buford informed me then that he had a friend who once sold tents to Billy Graham. This tent dealer had offered to make him a tent at a greatly discounted price.

When I left Buford, I texted Caroline. When we got on the phone, we talked for quite a while about other things before I mentioned that I'd found a good deal on a tent that fit all of my specifications. She promptly said, "My family would like to help with the tent." I wasn't sure what sort of help she was offering, so I asked what she meant. "We want to pay for it," she said.

"The whole tent?" I asked.

"Yes," she said. Caroline explained that her family had considerable financial resources, and they often make contributions when "God leads us" to worthwhile causes. I was stunned and grateful beyond words, of course. Certainly God was leading all of us in this cause.

As I am writing this, our big top is under construction with a delivery date to be determined. We have a lot of work to do and more funds to raise to buy seating and a sound system, but arrangements are swiftly falling into place. We've even identified several prospective sites for our first series of tent services in California.

I have felt convicted in my heart and have been saying for years that we need to have mass prayer efforts every day in America. Once we've pitched the tent for the first time, my plan is to have thirty days of prayer, just prayer, maybe a little music, with as many people as we can pack into it. I've also been in talks with groups like Teen Challenge and Brian Barcelona's One Voice to make the most of this new venue. I'm excited for all the opportunities that await us.

MAKE DISCIPLES OF ALL NATIONS

I've been asked to plant churches many times, but at this stage of my life, at least, I prefer to focus on outreach. My big tent is an effort to try a new way of reaching those who might feel more comfortable there than in a church. The huge venue also serves as a symbol for my long-term goal of bringing believers of all denominations under one tent, regardless of differing doctrines and traditions. This is my greater vision: to bring all who love God together, to overcome skepticism, ego, doubt, and stubbornness, and to focus on what should be our shared priority—the mission Jesus set for every Christian awaiting His return and the final reckoning: "Go therefore and make disciples of all nations, baptizing them in the name of the Father and of the Son and of the Holy Spirit, teaching them to observe all that I have commanded you. And behold, I am with you always, to the end of the age" (Matthew 28:19–20).

All Christians believe that the Son of God will return one day to vanquish Satan and welcome into heaven all those who have accepted Jesus Christ as their Savior. We all believe in serving others and following His commandments. My dream is that we can come together on common ground and make a massive effort to invite as many nonbelievers as we can into God's tent.

This is especially important now, in a time when overall church attendance is dropping, according to the Pew Research Center. Nearly a fourth of the US adult population now identifies as atheist or agnostic or claims no particular religion, according to Pew, and their numbers have risen 16 percent since 2007. The research organization also reported that between 2007 and 2014, the number of people surveyed who said they were Christians dropped from 78 percent to 71 percent.*

An army divided is an army conquered, as my uncle Batta likes to say. Christians of all denominations and nondenominations must unite. We have to accept that being a follower of Christ isn't about a church brand, one pastor's vision over another's, or whose doctrine is correct. It is about the power of the Holy Spirit and the love of God the Father and His Son.

We must focus on the fact that we have one primary mission on earth. Once you see the Lord is good and experience His love and peace, you want everyone else to experience it. No single Christian church or pastor owns the key to eternal salvation. That key is in God's hands. Our job is to get as many to His door as we possibly can while we serve Him here, and to do that, we need to join forces for the greatest of goods.

Ephesians 4:11–13 says, "It was [Christ] who gave some to be apostles, some to be prophets, some to be evangelists, and some to be pastors and teachers, to prepare God's people for works of service, so that the body of Christ may be built up until we all reach unity in the faith and in the knowledge of the Son of God and become mature, attaining to the whole measure of the fullness of Christ" (NIV). Our mission is to reach the lost, and we can reach more of them if we work together. What more power we would have if all Christian churches pooled their resources and acted as one mighty recruiting machine for God's army!

* Pew Research Center: Religion and Public Life, "America's Changing Religious Landscape," May 12, 2015, www.pewforum.org/2015/05/12/americas-changing-religious-landscape.

For too long those of us who share the same basic beliefs have all but shunned each other. As it is now, few American churches even talk to one another. Many churches have outreach programs, but unified action is rare, and as a result, there is no way to track progress or the lack of it.

THE NEED FOR MORE COMPASSION AND SERVICE

A pastor friend told me that his daughter adopted an African child who has been through hell. The child had suffered abuse and abandonment and needed professional counseling, but they couldn't find a faith-based counseling organization to help her overcome her depression, fear, and trauma. They finally turned to a secular program in another state, which was costly.

The pastor's daughter asked a question that has occurred to me as well: Why aren't our churches providing the services so desperately needed in our communities? It used to be that we turned to our churches in times of need. But the idea of serving a community no longer seems to be a priority for many churches. Too often they seem to be fixated on growing membership and acquiring property to build bigger and bigger church buildings.

If I were a pastor, I would want my congregation and my community to come to me first. I would want my church to be the ultimate social service agency, not just for my members, but for anyone who needed assistance. I was so moved by the story of the pastor's daughter and her adopted child that I spent several hours compiling a list of more than one hundred pains or needs that churches in every community should serve by cooperating and pooling their resources.

I live in Ventura County, California, where there are more than one hundred churches. Can you imagine the healing work they could do if they all joined forces to create a network of drug counselors, psychiatrists, counselors, nurses, physicians, financial advisors, tax experts, and other service providers for their congregation and nearby communities? Why do we think governments should bear all the burden? Isn't healing and helping the needy God's work?

In Matthew 9:28–29, we are told about Jesus entering a house where blind men came to Him for healing. Jesus asked them, "Do you believe that I am able to do this?" The blind men said they believed in His healing powers. Jesus then touched their eyes and said, "According to your faith be it done to you."

Jesus is compassionate. He stands at the door and waits for us to open it so He can love and heal us all. He loves strangers and even His enemies. I believe that all churches should show the same level of compassion by doing as much as they can to heal and assist anyone and everyone who comes to them. We shouldn't expect anyone else to do His work for us.

Churches need to serve the faithful and the unsaved. This is a form of outreach, a method for bringing more of God's children to His flock by serving their needs and showing them God's compassion. The world says I am disabled without hands and legs, but to me, a church that doesn't seek people to help and then give them all they need to nourish their faith is a disabled church. If we want people to welcome Jesus Christ into their lives, we have to show them how He works in their lives.

MANY PARTS FORM ONE BODY

Jesus didn't tell us to build the biggest churches we could build. He told us to serve His children. I don't want to be a pastor with the biggest church in the country. I'll gladly do His work in a tent that is open to all in need of salvation. God told us to bring souls to Him. We need to think big only in that regard.

"The body is a unit, though it is made up of many parts; and though all its parts are many, they form one body. So it is with Christ. For we were all baptized by one Spirit into one body—whether Jews or Greeks, slave or free—and we were all given the one Spirit to drink" (1 Corinthians 12:12–13, NIV).

Our mission should be to reach all who are still in need of the drink that brings everlasting salvation. There are slightly more than 7 billion people on earth. It is estimated that Christians comprise 2.2 billion or 31.5 percent of that total, with Catholics making up 50 percent, Protestants and nondenominational churches comprising 37 percent, and Orthodox 12 percent. Muslims, with an estimated 1.6 billion members, are said to be the fastest growing religious group, and many expect their numbers to surpass the number of Christians in the coming years.*

Our work is cut out for us, but I know we can do it because I have seen diverse churches and congregations come together increasingly in recent years. I've been particularly impressed with the open-tent operations of Steve and Barbara Telzerow, pastors of the International Christian Fellowship in Ljubljana, Slovenia. Their church is small but their vision is large.†

A few years ago they invited me to speak at a national outreach they organized by bringing together seventeen Slovenian churches, including Protestants, Orthodox, and nondenominationals. More than seventeen thousand people attended from the country of only two million.

Steve is a big-tent guy too. Historically, the Christian churches in Slovenia did not work together and barely communicated with each other. Steve was moved by God to bring me there. He knew he needed all hands on deck. He began visiting pastors, building bridges, and mending fences. He brought forgiveness and reconciliation. Soon the pastors were meeting, fasting, and praying together. Now they have regular meetings and look to find ways to pool their resources and work together. They worked as a team to bring me in to talk about the gospel of Jesus Christ.

---

* Tom Heneghan, "'No Religion' Is World's Third-Largest Religious Group After Christians, Muslims According To Pew Study," *Huffington Post*, December 19, 2012, www.huffingtonpost.com/2012/12/18/unaffiliated-third-largest-religious-group-after-christians-muslims_n_2323664.html.

† See https://harvestnetinternational.com/calendar/missions-conference/missionaries.

They are at a stage in Slovenia where they have a team and can all sit down and talk about mobilizing their seventeen churches and evangelizing together. They can find agreement on how to disciple converts and see them grow and expand. They are hoping to double the number of evangelical believers there. One of the first things Slovenian students are taught when they begin their schooling is a greeting attributed to Primoz Trubar, the first superintendent of the Slovenian Protestant Church: "I hope you know the truth of the knowledge of Jesus." So there is a long history of sharing the faith in that country.

A PRAYER WITH A PRESIDENT

On my 2016 trip to Slovenia, my inspirational speech to five thousand students was broadcast to every middle and high school in the country. They all stopped classes and watched as I was introduced by the president of Slovenia, Borut Pahor.

Since the government was sponsoring my appearance, I had to stick to inspirational rather than evangelical themes, but in my private hour-and-a-half meeting with the president, I shared the gospel with him. He wanted to pray for his country, so he got down on his knees. We prayed for the United States too. We were both very moved. He noted this was the first time a visitor had prayed with him in that office.

Steve Telzerow of the International Christian Fellowship was also present. He mentioned that 2017 is the five hundredth anniversary of the Reformation, and President Pahor said he would like to be the primary sponsor of events honoring that date.

Later I spoke about my love for Jesus Christ to more than four hundred people at an event organized by Steve and Barbara and their ministry. That event was videotaped and rebroadcast, so it reached thousands of Slovenians too. I was also the guest on a national television show for a forty-five-minute interview in which the hostess admitted that, until recently, she didn't understand what it meant to have faith. Then, to prepare for our interview, she read my book *Unstoppable,* and she told me, "It saved my life."

Wow! That was wonderful to hear, especially on a television show broadcast throughout Slovenia. She told me that my book helped her realize that faith isn't simply a philosophy but rather a belief and a way of living according to our belief in the Lord Jesus Christ as our Savior.

She finished my book and sought healing, restoration, and God's plan for her life. She'd been suffering from heartache, and God stepped in and filled the void. She was moved by the experience and expressed it beautifully. The interview was pretty awesome, one of the deepest on faith that I've ever done on a national television show.

I'm relating my Slovenia experiences because they demonstrate the benefits of Christians of all kinds working together under one tent. Steve and Barbara had no idea their efforts to bring me to Slovenia would result in such a meaningful meeting with the leader of their country and a television interview that proved to be one of the most compelling I've ever done on the power of faith. It's all about building momentum.

When we all work together to share our beliefs, God steps in and does more for us than we could ever have dreamed possible. I believe this is because He wants to encourage us to put aside petty differences and opinions and focus on the far more important mission of saving nonbelievers and delivering their souls to the gates of heaven.

PROCLAIMING FAITH SO OTHERS MIGHT HEAR

I have also seen the power of Christian unity at work in my adopted country. Among the notable efforts I've witnessed firsthand are those of Proclaim, a nonprofit organization with the mission of bringing churches together for the benefit of the communities in Madison County, Indiana.

Church leaders Gary Godbey, Bill Obras, Brad Henderson, and other big-tent Christians began the organization as an outreach event ministry.

Proclaim and its members are dedicated to the Great Commission. As my friend Jay Harvey, senior pastor of the Pendleton Christian Church, told me, "They bring communities together to see that the good news is indeed good."

They worked for several years to organize a community Easter service event, where I was honored to speak. Members of fifteen churches in the area participated. Everyone agreed that something unique happened that day. They actually held two services to accommodate the overflow crowds of more than fifteen thousand. Some had to watch it on a big screen in a high school gymnasium because they didn't have enough seats. Nearly a thousand gave their hearts to Jesus that day, according to estimates.

I will let Pastor Harvey tell you about that day. More importantly, he also will share his own journey of faith, which came late in his life, thanks to his love of basketball, which is the second largest religion in Indiana, I'm told!

> When Nick took the stage at the Easter event, I was immediately drawn in by his humor. This was the first time I had ever seen or heard of Nick. Most speakers are under the assumption they need to start with something funny or tell a joke to get the crowd warmed up, and that always makes me nervous. You can be a great speaker and communicator of the gospel but not know how to be funny or tell a joke. Not Nick! His self-deprecating humor and storytelling were so good; it was as if we were all just sitting in his living room and listening to this man of God share his heart.
>
> When Nick and I first worked together, it was at the request of Gary Godbey (president of Proclaim) who had kept a relationship with Nick. At this time, I had become the senior pastor of a large church in Pendleton, Indiana, where Gary attended. My story and

my style of communicating the gospel were a perfect fit to help Nick with his efforts to reach students all across the state of Indiana with his antibullying tour called Stand Strong.

Nick and I have developed a very solid and trusting relationship. When I am asked to work with Nick and help him in the schools or in the prisons, I simply serve him any way I can. I believe in what he is doing, but better yet, I believe in who he is as a person.

I did not grow up in the church. In fact, I only went when it meant I could play on the church basketball team. I found myself like so many others in this life, searching for something but not realizing it was Jesus.

At age thirty I was married with two children when my wife and kids and I began attending a church. I heard the gospel and kept coming back and needing more of what I now know was the goodness of God and His call to come. I surrendered after a couple of years and gave my whole life to Jesus and was baptized. I was delivered from drinking alcohol. I haven't had a drink since being baptized on April 25, 1999.

I have been a pastor for more than five years, but I have been writing and speaking for more than ten years. My ministry and my calling is to serve the church only in the way that helps them understand they have a responsibility to be people who reconcile, forgive, and love in a way that is foreign to the rest of the world.

When the body of Christ comes together through a parachurch ministry born of God and people seeking God, there is no denying the fruit that comes about. As a pastor, I love having this so close to me and knowing I can count on Proclaim ministries to help me come alongside other ministries and reach more people through Christ. Proclaim is powerful. Proclaim is of God, and Proclaim is changing lives.

IT IS TIME FOR A FRESH APPROACH

I've shared these inspiring stories with you because I believe my friends in Slovenia and Indiana are doing vitally important work: namely, God's mission. I believe we need an honest assessment of the state of Christianity today. The children in God's house must not be divided.

I'm for all denominations and for all who are nondenominational. I'm for the gospel and the kingdom of heaven. We need each other, all of us. We are told in 1 Corinthians 12:12: "For just as the body is one and has many members, and all the members of the body, though many, are one body, so it is with Christ."

We are all baptized by one Spirit. A few verses later, the apostle says, "If the foot should say, 'Because I am not a hand, I do not belong to the body,' that would not make it any less a part of the body. And if the ear should say, 'Because I am not an eye, I do not belong to the body,' that would not make it any less a part of the body" (verses 15–16).

We are all part of the body of Christ, and the earthly version of that body is in slow decline in the United States. Membership in mainline Protestant churches decreased from about forty-one million in 2007 to thirty-six million in 2014, according to the Pew Research Center. Today, the average age in their congregations is fifty-two and growing older. In the Catholic Church, the decline is even greater. It has lost three million members in the last decade. Seminaries and divinity schools also are losing enrollment, and many are shutting down.*

I fear that unless we follow the examples I've provided, we will lose the next generation of believers and spiritual leaders. We need to reorganize and rethink and reignite our efforts to bring nonbelievers to Jesus Christ.

Many churches are doing wonderful work, yet all too often they seem

* Pew Research Center: Religion and Public Life, "America's Changing Religious Landscape," May 12, 2015, www.pewforum.org/2015/05/12/americas-changing-religious-landscape.

to be focused internally rather than externally. They are so intent on protecting their turf or enforcing doctrine or building the largest empires that they neglect the critical mission. They are insular, not open. They are self-sustaining, not God serving.

There is not enough teaching of the gospel. Too many churches push fellowship without doing enough evangelism of nonbelievers and mentoring of new believers or Christians who have yet to establish intimate, personal relationships with God. Too many are adept at recruiting new members while failing to retain a strong core from one generation to the next. Too many churches have transactional relationships with their members instead of transformational relationships.

Church membership is dwindling. The nonbelievers are not coming, so we must go after them. We have to provide them with the information, motivation, and inspiration each step of the way. We can't just lure them in and then expect them to stay engaged. We must give them all the support and encouragement necessary to build a solid and lasting foundation of faith. We must help them stay on the path throughout their lives.

My philosophy for nurturing Christians is this:

- A healthy church understands the importance of reaching the lost and believers by going to them.
- We must teach, nurture, and support them one on one as unique individuals as they begin their walk with God.
- We must show maturing believers how to sustain faith by reading Scripture so they can build their personal relationships with God throughout their lives.
- We must teach the teachers and lead the leaders of the next generation of Christians.
- We must serve the entire community, just as Jesus did, with love for all.
- We must create worship atmospheres that feed the spirit and the soul without compromising on the Word of God.

- The Christian community should strive to become the greatest source of hope and assistance in every neighborhood, town, state, and nation.
- Our churches are not social clubs. They are the field command headquarters for God's army, and as such, they should be the most inclusive, nonjudgmental, welcoming, and focused source of spiritual guidance in the world.

After the Last Supper, Jesus offered a farewell to the eleven disciples who remained. In the final part of that farewell address on the night before His death on the cross, Jesus prayed to His Father for unity among the disciples: "May all be one, just as you, Father, are in me, and I in you, that they also may be in us."

He is our Father and we are His children, and we must find ways to serve Him together despite our differences. I know that when I watch my sons fight over their toys, it hurts me. I want them to play together and love and support each other in the house we all share. I'm sure it hurts our heavenly Father when His Christian children bicker and shun each other.

We need to give the Holy Spirit a chance to guide us. We are instruments in His hands. Instead of focusing on our differences, we need to unite on common ground. Jesus saved us. He is Lord. There are lost people out there. We need to join forces as Christians and find ways to reach out to those lost souls and save them. We must go out to the four corners of the world and make disciples of them all.

THE GREAT COMMISSION

I have this recurring dream that one day I will be standing before God, and He will ask me two questions.

The first: "Do you know Me?"

The second: "Who did you bring with you?"

I think the first question is asked to establish a Christian identity. The second is to see if I've done what is the primary mission of all Christians on earth. In Matthew 28:18, the resurrected Jesus stood on a mountain in Galilee and commanded His followers to go forth and baptize all nations in the name of the Father, the Son, and the Holy Spirit. He also told us in Mark 16:15 to "Go into all the world and proclaim the gospel to the whole creation."

This direction from Jesus Christ, our risen Savior, is known as the Great Commission. I've made it my mission, and I encourage every Christian I meet and every church I visit to keep it as a central purpose each and every day. A large church once asked me how to crack the code and get more members to join. They asked me in particular if I knew of an effective teacher who was reaching members of the younger generation and drawing them into worship services in large numbers.

Shortly after that, another church leader told me that their growth had suddenly leveled off after a couple of years of rapid expansion. This pastor also wondered how to grow and retain members.

My response to both church leaders was that I was not interested in numbers. I'm interested in souls. I believe our primary mission as Christians shouldn't be to build the biggest churches and pack them with believers. My goal is to reach nonbelievers and those who haven't yet heard the good news.

My encouragement to pastors everywhere is to come under one tent to fulfill this primary mission, the Great Commission. I don't mean just my tent, of course. But my big top will serve as an example for other believers interested in working together.

Many church leaders have shared frustrations with me because they don't know how to reach those yet to accept Jesus Christ as their Savior. They struggle to empower their church members to share their faith outside its walls. Too many members feel their responsibility is simply to attend services from week to week in order to have their spirits fed. I would encourage them to go out and break bread with nonbelievers at every opportunity.

To help the churches that are looking for ways to bring more of God's children into His flock, I have created the nine keys of the Great Commission. These are merely suggestions based on my experiences of telling people about Jesus and making as many disciples as I can.

1. Reach the lost and teach them how to evangelize.

When I first gave my life to Jesus, I wanted to tell the world, *Jesus lives!* The peace I felt was incredible. I felt restoration in my soul, and for the first time, I knew the truth of my purpose and identity. I knew my destiny in God was bigger than anything I could ever imagine or attain.

All Christians should feel that excited about sharing their faith, and all churches should work together in reaching out to those who have yet to find faith. They need to understand that there are no barriers to entry. When Jesus comes into our lives, He takes care of all guilt and addiction. There is no condemnation for those who encourage others to accept Jesus. We want everyone to know God loves them.

There is no greater purpose for us than getting to know God and loving God with all of our might, our souls, and our spirits. The second greatest purpose is to love our neighbors as ourselves. You show that love by helping them identify their values and purpose and destiny.

2. Teach believers to feed themselves: read, study, and pray.

This isn't really about actually feeding people; it is about creating an army of the faithful to recruit and serve those who've yet to welcome Jesus Christ into their lives. It's strange that many Christian churches have common goals but rarely talk to each other, and it is even more rare for them to work together toward those goals.

3. Serve the community.

I often think that Christian churches are among the most dysfunctional community of faith in the world. I'll go into a county with eighty churches, and instead of all or most of them cooperating on community efforts, maybe three or four are doing something together, such as operating food pantries. Think how much more effective they could be and how many more souls could be brought to Jesus if they all worked together!

4. Teach beginner believers.

Churches rarely unite to support and serve people once they've proclaimed their faith. They don't continue to nurture those new recruits and help them mature in faith. You can't expect someone who answers an altar call on Sunday to immediately have a deep understanding of the responsibilities and blessings that come with being a Christian. One sermon a week won't cut it. There has to be a bridge for beginners and intermediate Christians so they can grow in their understanding of God's Word.

5. Teach believers to feed others.

Those of us who grew up in strong Christian families are fortunate because our parents helped nurture us in the faith by reading the Bible to us and explaining the meaning of scriptures. They also served as mentors and role models in the way they lived the Ten Commandments. This homeschooling plants in us the desire to feed others who are hungry for God's Word. Churches need to be actively engaged in creating the next generation of Christian guides, mentors, and role models, and they can do that most effectively by working together.

6. Create a compelling worship atmosphere.

I grew up in a very traditional church, and we sang hymns that were part of those rich traditions, though some of the younger people didn't think they were very exciting. The idea of worship is to praise God, and we do that by singing to magnify His excellence. We are exulting in Him, worshipping Him, and thanking Him by telling God we love Him as a family of believers.

I don't want that purpose to be lost or buried. I worry that some churches get caught up in competing with each other over which of them can be more pious and more demonstrative rather than focusing on loving God, sharing that love, and passing it on.

Everyone has a preference when it comes to worship services. I believe we all want to experience intimacy and growth with God. When we come together to worship Him, I believe God takes extra delight. He inhabits the praise of His people. I think worshipping together gives us a glimpse of heaven. Heaven will be about worshipping God face to face as the Author of our faith.

7. Deploy the talents of disciples.

I encourage church leaders to look at their congregation as an army of evangelists with a wealth of knowledge, talents, and gifts that should be identified and deployed in the world. How many great recruiters are out there? How many know the gospel and can teach it in compelling ways? How many counselors, good listeners, and encouragers are there in each church? We need to make the most of our human resources and tap their talents to build God's own army.

8. Become the biggest free resource in the community.

I urge church leaders in every community to pool their efforts to become the largest provider of resources to those in need, whether it is food pantries, marriage counseling, antibullying programs, suicide-prevention programs, youth activities, programs for seniors, fitness classes, childcare, or other possible offerings. What better way to share our faith than to share our blessings with those who may not yet know the joy and fulfillment of our Christian lives?

9. Take care of our real mission.

Some pastors want to be businessmen. They develop a corporate CEO mentality that focuses on constant growth. They focus on making their churches bigger, as if it were a competition. It is not a competition. I believe sound nonprofit business practices should be followed in the operation of any church when it comes to finances and employees, but a church is not a business. It is God's house, and church leaders need to be focused on inviting as many into it as possible and then making sure they are comfortable enough to stay around for eternity.

10

ADVENTURES IN FAITH

I have traveled three million miles around the world over the last fifteen years, speaking to more than six hundred million people in person or via television simulcasts in more than sixty-three countries. I've also had the honor to meet with sixteen presidents, prime ministers, and other heads of state.

I may not be in the country for the specific purpose of sharing my faith, although that never stops me from my most important mission. I am always searching for ways to reach out to those who might be looking for a path to heaven, and I let everyone know that I am willing to guide them to Jesus Christ. I do have to be careful when I'm in countries that are not hospitable to Christians or evangelists in general. The coordinators and promoters who bring me into such venues are putting their necks on the line, so I have to stick to our agreements to protect them. I don't want to be responsible for anyone being punished because of something I've said or done. I try not to breach their trust and faith in me.

If the government hosting us doesn't want me to talk about my faith, I generally don't—unless someone asks me during a Q&A or in a media interview. Once I'm asked a question, usually I'm free to answer it. I may sometimes hint that it would be okay to ask me certain questions. Then I'll take the opportunity to do a little faith sharing.

In 2008 I was asked by Chinese officials to speak to college students for a suicide-prevention campaign. After my speech, I opened the meeting to questions from the audience. A student asked me about being a Christian. As I replied, another person started weeping loudly and cried out, "How can you love a God who gave you a life of pain without arms or legs?"

The perfect question! I responded as I always do. I told him and the other students that none of us are perfect. We are all cracked or broken in some way. The answer is to put our broken and cracked pieces in the hands of God. I believe that His design for us will then be revealed over time.

I found my purpose in a life without limbs. God guided me to lead a life without limits. My lack of limbs has provided me with a platform, an entry point, into conversations about God and faith and hope. I learned that while God may not give me the miracle I've sought by giving me limbs, He has put me in position to be a miracle in the lives of many other people.

My mission isn't about getting limbs for myself; it's about helping people redeem and restore their lives so they can live with purpose and truth and accept Jesus Christ as their Savior.

I take those opportunities as teaching moments, but again, I try not to get anyone in trouble or offend anyone. In Paraguay, I did a little preaching when I wasn't supposed to, and a person in the audience called out, "Can we make sure that we never let him or anybody else talk about God again?"

Wow, that was not a typical response! Usually when someone is aggravated or tries to bait me into a political debate or attacks my faith, I take the diplomatic route. I tell them that God loves them just as He loves us all, and I promise to pray for them. Love conquers all!

Often I'm invited to talk to adolescents and teens about the dangers of bullying or to tell them that suicide is not an option because God loves them and is always there for them. Sometimes I am invited into a country to serve as an advocate for the disabled.

No matter why I'm there, I always ask my audiences and the officials I meet with to pray with me or to let me pray for them. This has led to some very interesting conversations, including an especially notable one with the president of Macedonia that I will describe later in this chapter.

GOING TO THE TOP

I never know how a meeting with a head of state will go. Sometimes they are warm and sincerely interested in sharing their beliefs and thoughts. At other times they are more distant and perfunctory and not at all inclined to have a two-way conversation. I get it. These are very important and busy people with incredible responsibilities and complex matters on their minds. They don't have time to idly chat with visitors.

Usually they are willing to spend a small part of their schedule with me if they are familiar with my videos and my books. Several have told me they first learned about me when their children showed them my books, videos on YouTube, or my Facebook page.

The president of Hungary, János Áder, and his wife, Anita Herczegh, who have three daughters and a son, were among those whose children introduced them to my work. I met with them in 2013 as part of my World Outreach tour through twenty-six countries, and I could immediately feel their genuine love and concern for their country. We had a deep conversation about their love of God and their desire to serve their people with His help.

They came across as smart, as well as very pure of heart and authentic. They acknowledged that they needed God, and that is the beginning of wisdom, knowing He is real and that we need Him and should honor Him in everything we do so that He will bless us in return.

Of course, not every head of state is a Christian, but I'm grateful to meet those who aren't if they give me an opportunity to serve as a positive example for them and their citizens. When they are willing to spend more than a few minutes with me, I've found that our conversation can be deep and even quite moving. Occasionally, though, they will leave me shaking my head, trying to figure out what just happened.

TOUGH TIMING

It's entirely possible in those instances that they were talking over my head or just trying to give me a glimpse of what was in their heads. That was the case when I met with Macedonia's president, Gjorge Ivanov, in the spring of 2016. I was grateful for this opportunity, especially because I've always wanted to spend more time in Macedonia, a beautiful and historic country that, like Serbia, was a former republic of Yugoslavia.

Still, the timing was not the best for this visit. There was a great deal of turmoil in the country at the time. Just two days before I arrived, violence broke out between the security forces and hundreds of migrants and refugees who were trying to break through a fence along the country's border with Greece.

Then, on the next day, there were riots in the nation's capital, Skopje, by demonstrators upset that President Ivanov had pardoned fifty-six officials and politicians who were under investigation for allegedly wiretapping twenty thousand citizens and other crimes. Protestors even ransacked the president's office and tried, unsuccessfully, to set it on fire. (He later rescinded the pardons.)

This made me more than a little nervous, of course. I was there for the biggest evangelical outreach ever attempted in Macedonia, where Orthodox Christians are the largest religious group, followed by Muslims, who are almost one-third of the population. We'd heard reports that many government officials and journalists were suspicious of evangelists and wary of what I would say in my speech.

I've known some Macedonians, and they can be tough-minded and skeptical because they have a long history of hardship. With all the upheaval in his country and the criticism of his pardons, I expected President Ivanov would cancel our meeting. But he didn't.

During our meeting, there were about five thousand protestors on the steps of the capitol. This atmosphere and the reception I received from President Ivanov provided quite a contrast to our previous stop in Serbia. There I'd been welcomed by a top official who shared a very similar last name, Prime Minister Aleksandar Vucic. (No *j* in his last name and no relation that I know of.)

Prime Minister Vucic and I had an engaging, open, and frank conversation, a wonderful time, and one of the best meetings I've ever had with a head of state. We talked about the Serbian education system, the political winds in the West, and the challenges of being a leader in the modern world. I was impressed with his humility and warmth.

We talked for a solid hour and had a very real conversation. He talked about the importance of educating young people and sparking entrepreneurship in Serbia. He also reflected on the challenges of being a leader. I haven't agreed with every decision he's made in office, but his beliefs seem to come from the heart rather than his ego. He had tears in his eyes while thanking me for praying for Serbia and inspiring its young people, and I was equally moved.

A LEARNING EXPERIENCE

My hour-long meeting with President Ivanov was quite different. He acted like a professor delivering a lecture, which makes sense—he has a PhD, once led a law school's political studies department, and has lectured at universities around the world, including Yale Divinity School in the United States. Maybe I should have raised my hand to get in a word, because there was no give-and-take in our conversation.

He spent the entire time in lecture mode, talking about his life and his philosophy. He stressed that I needed to expand my spiritual base of knowledge beyond reading the Bible and Christian texts.

President Ivanov promotes religious diversity, and he shared with me his philosophy about the benefits of speaking to nature, including rocks and trees. He said I should stop reading and talking about the Bible and spend more time talking to nature, because it would make me a better person and bring good karma. He seemed to imply that the only reason I was a Christian was because I didn't know any better.

That pushed me over the edge. I finally spoke up, "With all due respect, sir, I'm trying to give hope to women living in slums. I think it is more helpful to tell them about God's love and the possibility of redemption than to suggest they talk to trees. Their parents sold them into sex slavery when they were children. They haven't known much hope."

He went quiet for a few moments and then switched gears and launched into a random lecture about the Orthodox Church and how its members no longer understood how to tap the power of prayer. He had consulted with Orthodox priests about this, and they'd agreed that about four hundred years ago, people stopped saying "amen" properly and thus lost the power of prayer.

I am not making this up. Macedonia's top official then went into a lengthy explanation of the proper way to say "amen" so that you tap into the full power of prayer. I tried not to laugh as he kept repeating, in varying forms, but always in a loud chanting voice, *Ahhhhh-MEEEE—nnnnnn!*

I struggled to keep a straight face as President Ivanov stressed that a proper "amen" had to be stretched out and said at exactly 539 decibels in order to fully harness its power to reach God's ear. For some reason, this made me wonder what would happen if I said "amen" just a few decibels higher. Would pigeons begin to fall out of the sky?

The embattled leader seemed to think he was enlightening me with his wealth of knowledge, and I didn't try to convince him otherwise. Despite my alleged lack of wisdom and worldliness and my refusal to talk to shrubs, he invited me to speak at his youth leadership camp one day. He noted that a previous guest speaker was the Dalai Lama. I wondered if the Tibetan Buddhist leader had received the same lecture on how to say "amen" properly. Probably not.

In the end, President Ivanov allowed me to say a prayer for him, and he thanked me for coming to his country to talk about God. I am grateful also that he invited me to speak to his youth camp, just as I welcome every opportunity to share my faith, whether with world leaders in their ornate (if slightly charred) offices or orphaned children in the poorest corners of the earth.

GO INTO ALL THE WORLD AND PREACH

My global adventures in faith haven't always been enjoyable. Sometimes they've been scary. I return home exhausted physically from most of my trips, but I am mentally and spiritually fired up because doing God's work is such a thrill for me. Whenever I receive an invitation to meet with a president or prime minister, it's icing on the cake—and a potential opportunity to make an impact, however small.

First, I assume there is only a 50 percent chance the meeting will actually happen. They are, after all, very busy people. I try to respect their time. Often our meetings are brief and little more than a photo opportunity or a meet and greet, but occasionally I've been moved by these high-level meetings. On a few of these encounters, I even dare to think maybe I've opened the door to God's influence.

In Liberia in 2008, I met with my first president: Ellen Johnson Sirleaf. She was educated at Harvard and became the first woman elected to lead an African nation. Her leadership has taken Liberia many steps forward from a past dominated by warlords, violence, and corruption. In 2011 she shared the Nobel Peace Prize with two others (Tawakel Karman of Yemen and fellow Liberian Leymah Gbowee).

During our 2008 meeting, we had a deep and meaningful conversation and prayed for each other. She thanked me in particular for helping to raise awareness in a region where many children born with disabilities were murdered or abandoned. I was quite impressed with her, and I believed she wanted to improve the lives of her people.

One of my most moving and rewarding encounters with a national leader occurred in 2013 in Ecuador, when I met with President Rafael Correa at the Carondelet Palace. I was one of several guests of honor who stood by him, high on the steps of the palace, for a ceremony. It was basically a one-minute meeting with a one-minute prayer. I wasn't given an opportunity to speak at length with him, but something clicked between us.

At the time, there was political pressure on President Correa, a Catholic and an economist who was educated in the United States, to legalize abortion in his country. Some of it stemmed from the prevalence of rapes in Ecuador.

There were forces within the president's own governing alliance pushing for legalization. During the ceremony, teens demonstrated and held up signs for abortion rights. I'd seen news reports of prochoice advocates saying women should have the right to abort children with disabilities.

It was a very sensitive and volatile issue in Ecuador, but I did not discuss this with the president. I only said I would pray for him and his country. I looked into his eyes and said I would like to pray for him to be blessed and that I loved him and thanked him for allowing me to come into his country to influence his young people.

He consented to the prayer. As I said it, I watched to see if he bowed his head, something I always do when I offer a prayer for heads of state. If they bow their heads and close their eyes, I believe they are sincere in wanting my prayer. It also shows they aren't afraid to close their eyes in public, which is not an infallible indicator but more of a fluid measure of how genuine they are in their walk with Christ.

When I finished praying, I opened my eyes and hugged him. A photo was taken, and that was it. Nine days later he made a public statement saying that as long as he was president, abortion would not be legalized and that he would resign if the national assembly acted to legalize abortion without his agreement.

In a report about his decision, President Correa said he was against any effort to allow abortions of babies expected to have disabilities because, "after meeting with Nick Vujicic," he thought that his country could do with a lot more people like me.

Wow, if ever I doubted the importance of being a role model and striving to live without limits, this certainly serves as a reminder. I think the president saw me as an example of what even someone with severe disabilities can do in this world.

There have been other times when I've felt like my meetings with heads of state were only token affairs and photo opportunities for political reasons rather than to have a thoughtful exchange of ideas. Sometimes when I'm scheduled for only a brief meeting with a president or prime minister, I've wondered what God's plan might be.

My experience in Ecuador offered an answer to that. You never know the impact you can have on someone simply by walking in faith and serving as a wholesome example of God's goodness and kindness. I don't know for certain that I had any impact on the president's decision to speak out against abortion in his country. He is a Catholic and a highly principled man, after all. Yet maybe I helped give him strength and a greater sense of purpose on this issue.

When I heard he'd mentioned me as a positive influence, I rejoiced and thanked God for putting me in a position to do His work once again. I also vowed to never again underestimate His power to influence others through me. It is a humbling thing, but I believe God put me there on that day for a reason, just as He had put me on earth to serve His purposes. The same is true for you! I encouraged you to open yourself to God's presence in your life. Ask Him each and every day what you can do to serve Him.

As a side note, President Correa was elected to a second five-year term. He left office in 2017 after serving his country for ten years as president. I saw a news account that reported on his decade in office. "Ecuador has lifted more than 1.5 million people out of poverty, doubled the minimum wage, doubled health spending per person, cut unemployment by over 4 percent and expanded social security to hundreds of thousands of people for the first time, among other social and economic gains." I don't take any credit for President Correa's decisions or his successes; only the man himself and God deserve that.*

As God's servant, I want to bring as many others to the gates of heaven as I can. My travels also are explorations. Everywhere I go, I look for those in the greatest need of God's love. I seek out those who are neglected or even abused by their governments. I pray for them and also try to influence change by walking through the corridors of power and lobbying leaders to do more for the neediest of their people.

My hope is to bring God's presence into their offices so He can influence them. I believe God puts me in every meeting, whether with a world leader or with anyone seeking a prayer, a word, a hug, or an introduction to the power of the Holy Spirit.

Honestly, when in the office of some heads of state, I swear I can smell corruption and see vanity and pride emanating from them. I may feel evil

* "Ecuador Celebrates 10 Years Of The Citizens' Revolution," *Neritam* (blog), March 8, 2017, https://jagadees.wordpress.com/2017/03/08/ecuador-celebrates-10-years-of-the-citizens-revolution.

in the room, but that is even more reason for me to be there, to introduce God's goodness and represent Him. I always present myself as an ambassador of the Lord.

I tell heads of state that my only mission is to help them know that God loves them and that we all need His strength and wisdom. I note that every decision should honor God, because if you honor Him, God will honor you.

I really believe a nation that honors God is a blessed nation. I have not come across any country that does not need healing at some level. We all need healing, we all need help, and we all need God. Unfortunately, we live in a world of people who can be selfish, prideful, and greedy.

I've turned down meetings with some leaders whom I felt were corrupt and wanted to use me to bolster their images among believers. Sometimes the risks are just too great if I don't think I can have a meaningful conversation and be a positive influence rather than risk being a token.

It is not my job to tell a president what to do or to judge the leader's decisions. I didn't scold the president of Macedonia for locking out refugees or pardoning those who abused their power. I came to him as I come to everyone, with love and respect. Still, I never forget my primary mission is to plant seeds of faith with the conviction of the Holy Spirit. I pray for the powerful to use their power wisely and benevolently. That is the mission of all Christians and citizens. Even if we complain about our leaders in private, they still need our prayers, because our nations need them to serve us well.

When photos are posted online of me with politicians I sometimes take flak from those who oppose them. I don't mean to endorse everything they do. I often don't agree with certain policies. So just because I'm seen with a president, a prime minister, or a mayor doesn't mean I endorse everything that official does. Jesus sought out prostitutes and criminals and sinners, not because He believed in their lifestyles, but because His mission on earth was to save lost souls and make the ultimate sacrifice for our sins.

I've had people tell me I shouldn't go to certain places because of the evil influences there, but I wear the armor of God. That doesn't mean I take unnecessary risks. I never travel alone. I have a team around me, and I have hundreds and even thousands praying for me. I know also that God's angels are with me and the Holy Spirit is living in me as well. I don't put myself in danger, but I do go into dark places to shine the light of Jesus and show the real hope to be found in Christ.

SERVING AS A STRONGHOLD

Living in the United States, and particularly California, might blind me to needs around the world if I hadn't seen so much of it for myself. There are many countries in which only the wealthy enjoy modern amenities and technology. Far too many people around the world are being left behind as those in power drain their country's resources. Even worse, those who have the power to assist the neediest refuse to do so.

In Montenegro, another former republic of Yugoslavia and country where my father's family has roots, the government does not allow churches or people to start their own nonprofit organizations. In the Balkan region, it is common that the governments tax nonprofits on each donation. This makes it difficult for these groups to provide assistance to the needy.

How do Christians influence nations and their leaders? We have to walk in faith into their capitals, pray for them, and ask the Holy Spirit to touch them and put them on a path to follow God's plan.

We can only do so much. We are the messengers and God does the rest. I try to be His ambassador by influencing, praying for, and talking to government leaders whenever the opportunity arises. I want to represent His goodness, love, and integrity wherever I go. Most of the time, people understand that and treat me well, but not all the time.

RUSSIA CONTROVERSY

I had a busy year in 2016 and even went to Russia for an inspirational speaking tour that included Yekaterinburg, Chelyabinsk, Sochi, Minsk, and the Kremlin in Moscow. Russia is one of several nations where discrimination against the disabled is still common. Ninety percent of its buildings do not have disabled access. Most public transportation is also inaccessible, including nearly all of Moscow's extensive subway system. Vladimir Putin's government has taken some steps to improve access to public buildings and transportation systems, but activists for the disabled are still highly critical of their treatment in Russia.

I'd been led to believe there might be an opportunity to meet with President Putin in Moscow. He has sought to make political points by championing his country's Paralympic athletes. I was eager to encourage him to extend his support to all of his nation's 12.7 million disabled citizens. I'd been to Russia a couple of times before, but this looked like a big chance to influence its most powerful leader. You never know until you try, right? Hope is everything!

Little did I know I would be rolling into a mighty storm of controversy. In fact, this storm whirled around me on an international scale, even though I was unaware of it at the time. On April 14, the day I arrived in Moscow, an editor for a pro-Putin radio and newspaper operation, Yevgeniy Arsyukhin, wrote an opinion piece about me that caused an international uproar—and I didn't hear about it until I returned home.

The title of the article was "Nick Vujicic and the Waiver of Evolution" (whatever that means). In the article, he seemed to suggest that disabled people like me should be put to death at birth, and if we were allowed to live, we should never be permitted to have children. There was also a line that translated into English as, "And we should never let disabled people get to the top of the social pyramid."

The author later claimed he was only stating what many had believed in the past and that these were not his personal beliefs. The BBC's online site reported, "In the piece, Arsyukhin—who is chief editor of the newspaper's sister radio station—presented his view of how society's attitude towards disabled people had changed over the centuries. 'Our disgust towards ugliness, sickness and to death is hardwired into us by evolution and natural selection,' he wrote, going on to add 'defective individuals should not produce offspring, it's better that they die straight away. And we should never let disabled people get to the top of the social pyramid.'"*

Arsyukhin wrote, "Aversion to 'physical deformity,' to disease, to death itself is embedded in us by evolution and natural selection," and "Ancient people considered it a necessity to kill a handicapped person in infancy. Disabled specimen should not survive or breed. It's best if they died right away."

He added, "Yet, some three thousand years ago, a colossal overturn took place in the minds of men—they challenged natural selection, not wishing to live by its law. . . . Jesus sealed this revolution. He put the poor above the successful once and for all. From now on, at least formally, sympathy for [the disabled] is an integral part of civilization."

To cap it all off, Arsyukhin appeared to take a shot at me for trying to inspire people. According to the BBC translation and report on the controversy, he wrote, "His fans enthusiastically repeat banalities like 'He gave us self-confidence, if he was able to become successful, we can and we will as well!' But deep down, they all—or almost all—feel pity and even disgust for their idol. . . . And there is nothing monstrous about it."

BACKLASH

I don't read Russian newspapers or listen to Russian radio. I don't speak or understand the language. So I missed the story and the huge backlash. I later learned the Russian promoter who'd brought me into the country

* Dmytro Zotsenko, *BBC Trending* (blog), "Russians Respond to 'Disabled Should Die Straight Away' Row," April 22, 2016, www.bbc.com/news/blogs-trending-36085624.

decided not to tell me about the controversy because he didn't want to upset me.

Meanwhile, my staff in the United States was fielding phone calls from reporters around the world, but since they hadn't heard from me, they said, "No comment," which was interpreted as "Nick wasn't offended."

The Russian columnist didn't hear from me, but he heard from plenty of other folks who wrote, called, and lambasted him on social media. Some called him a fascist and conducted an online petition campaign to have him fired. It was reportedly signed by more than ninety thousand people.

The article was removed from the website where he'd posted it. A disclaimer was posted in its place, saying the news outlet "respects the opinion of its readers." But it also said, "It became clear to us that many of the opponents did not read the full text, limiting at best, at a few paragraphs." Arsyukhin did a radio interview in which he said today's Internet-oriented readers are prone to read only headlines and summaries, while his article was purposely written in a "more complicated way," without solid conclusions, and had to be completely read to be fully understood, according to a BBC report.

Arsyukhin also apologized in the radio interview to those offended by his ideas, saying he didn't understand what other apologies the activists behind the petition could demand. The BBC translated his semi-apology as: "Bottom-line, this debate . . . draws attention to the problems of the disabled, but also draws negative attention to them. Perhaps, I was wrong to start it, at least in this form . . . but it turned out like that—thanks to the people with no brain that repost only the first paragraph, and do not read any further. So I apologize once and for all."

Honestly, after reading the media translations of the article and the author's strange apology, I didn't know what to make of it all. Maybe something was lost in the translation and Arsyukhin really was trying to show how times have changed for the better for the disabled in Russia, or maybe he was saying they *should* change for the better.

Whatever his intent, I forgave him and prayed for him. I also am grateful to all those who stood up for me. I suggest everyone who signed the petition make an effort to pass on a kindness to the next disabled person they meet. That would turn something potentially hurtful into something good, don't you agree?

A TROUBLING LAW

I still hope to one day meet with President Putin so I can make a case for greater accessibility and better treatment of the disabled in his country. I would also talk to him about keeping Russia open to Christian missionaries. He and his government have sent mixed signals in that regard. In his 2016 Orthodox Christmas address, Putin praised Christians for "reviving the high ethical, moral values, guarding our rich historical and cultural heritage" and for helping maintain civil peace.*

Yet earlier that year, in July, his government had passed legislation known as the Yarovaya Law, which resulted in a crackdown on foreign missionary work and evangelism in Russia. I'm told this law was created in part because some were not paying the required fees to hold religious meetings. The fees start at $750, so they are not overly expensive.

Within a few weeks, Russian police arrested Don Ossewaarde, a Baptist missionary from the United States, while he was holding a weekly Bible study and charged him under the new law that requires missionaries to have permits, limits religious activity to registered church buildings, and makes house churches illegal. Ossewaarde was found guilty and fined more than six hundred dollars.

When I last checked, there had been at least thirty-two other arrests and eighteen convictions of missionaries under the law for things like

* Sarah Eekhoff Zylstra, "US Missionary May Get Russia's Anti-Evangelism Law Overturned," January 24, 2017, www.christianitytoday.com/news/2017/january/us-missionary-may-get-russia-evangelism-law-overturned.html.

handing out New Testaments at a train station. Among those arrested were five Pentecostals, two Baptists, two Seventh-day Adventists, and four other Protestants, according to *Christianity Today* and other media reports.

As you would expect, I find this very troubling. Open discussions about spiritual beliefs are healthy and important. I agree that evangelists shouldn't try to force others to change what they believe, but it's not about that. The goal should be to open the door by explaining to those who are curious what else is out there and letting them make their own decisions.

Many atheists, Muslims, and Buddhists talk to me about their beliefs, and I love those dialogues. I'm confident in my beliefs and not threatened that there are those who espouse a different faith—unless they inhibit the rights or threaten the safety of others.

If you limit discussions on spirituality in a society or restrict a country to one faith or none at all, you risk eliminating hope for the people who are struggling or are underserved in a world where corruption and evil are powerful forces. Our souls are the most important part of us. When your soul is at peace in faith, you are more likely to be happy, fulfilled, and more inclined to serve others. That is what makes for a healthy society.

In Russia, Don Ossewaarde and others have filed appeals, and there are indications the country's supreme court may find the law violates the Russian constitution. Protests against the law have been registered by the Protestant churches of Russia, the European Evangelical Alliance, and the US Commission on International Religious Freedom. There are even media reports that President Putin allowed the law as a show of solidarity with the Russian Orthodox Church, but I don't know that for sure.

In the Balkans there are often walls between church and the government, but at the same time the school system still teaches orthodoxy and the saints and the faith, although it is often less about faith than about Russian identity and the history of the country.

I've been in discussions with the Russian Orthodox Church about conducting a national day of prayer in their country, and people on President

Putin's staff have indicated they want to arrange a meeting when I'm not in Moscow for a commercial speaking event. So this may eventually happen. I know his schedule is fluid and variable, but I'll take the risk to go and talk to him.

OUR SHARED MISSION

I would pray with President Putin for the Russian people and for an active relationship between God and them. My goal with him and all national leaders is to look them in the eye, get to know them, pray for them, and dialogue with them. If a nation or its leaders don't want me to give a speech on my faith, I will offer an inspirational message or a message on bullying in order to build relationships and make connections that will one day allow me to share or at least demonstrate my Christian beliefs. In the process, I prepare the path through which I hope to make disciples.

Creating relationships that open the door to faith sharing is also the mission of Encompass World Partners, which supports missionaries in thirty-four nations. I worked with Encompass in Southeast Asia to help a college student with Down syndrome. Children with disabilities are seen as a shame on their families in that part of the world. Parents are encouraged to abort or abandon babies with disabilities. Communities generally have very little in the way of a support system for those with special needs.

Encompass asked me to visit the community of this college student with Down syndrome. They said my speaking engagement opened the door to "sow further seeds of truth into their relationships" with people in the region.

I want to plant seeds of hope and truth for citizens of every country I visit. The controversy over the Russian column written about me and the new anti-evangelism law in that country certainly have done nothing to slow me down or make me abandon or even question my mission to serve as God's ambassador and recruiter wherever I go. That role also includes serving as an advocate and supporter for disabled people and all others who suffer around the world.

STAYING ON MISSION IN A DANGEROUS WORLD

I've been working on leveraging technology so I don't have to travel quite as much as I did in the past. When I was younger and single, traveling around the world was a kind of adventure. Now, with a wife and two boys at home, it's so difficult to leave them for extended periods of time. I miss them too much.

I want to continue to do God's work and to serve as a source of hope and inspiration to people everywhere, so I won't give up traveling entirely, but I do hope to cut back. My team and I have been working with simulcasts, podcasts, Skype broadcasts, and other tech tools, as well as all other forms of social media, to reach more and more people.

The world is more dangerous now, and that is another concern. I have had some close calls. Just one day after I left Mumbai in 2008, terrorists bombed three places we'd visited, including my hotel, the train station, and the airport. There have been many other less scary but still crazy traveling misadventures.

The Russia controversy reminded me of an "international incident" that arose without my knowledge during my 2013 visit to Vietnam. The promoter of my appearance in Ho Chi Minh City had hired private security guards to escort me from the airport to my hotel. They had motorbikes and cars with sirens, and they got a little carried away.

Basically, they stopped all traffic to clear the way for my vehicle, and they ran red lights and even drove in the wrong lanes—all of which was illegal. The police later fined them and seized several of their vehicles. The local media launched a big campaign to stop private security companies from being so aggressive.

Sorry, Ho Chi Minh City. Next time I'll just take Uber from the airport! I don't often use private security, but sometimes my hosts feel it is necessary. I believe that when God calls me to a place, He will make it safe for me. There is no safer place than where God wants us to be, not that I haven't had a scare or two.

One night I was traveling through Belgrade in Serbia when riots broke out over some government action. We were doing a mile trek around a big block in the city. When we started out, all was calm, but the rioters were right behind us, and we didn't even know it. By the time we came back around to our starting point, the entire area had been torn apart. Windows were smashed. Street lights were broken. Tables and chairs were thrown into the streets and on top of cars. Buildings were on fire. We were shocked. Calm had been replaced with chaos.

I said several prayers of thanks that none of us were hurt. Some said we were lucky, but I definitely think God was protecting us because we were doing His work.

FINDING INSPIRATION FROM OTHERS AROUND THE WORLD

There is one major benefit to traveling that will probably keep me on the road at least a few weeks a year. That benefit is *you*! I meet so many wonderful and inspiring people in my travels. I have made so many friends and learned so much from the people I meet at my speaking events as well as in hotels, restaurants, and airports. You all have made me feel so welcomed, so loved, and so much a part of God's family.

I am sincere about being inspired by you and by so many million joyful, faith-filled, God-loving people who have challenges far greater than mine.

There is nothing quite like rolling into an orphanage or a shelter for sex slaves and finding boys and girls, men and women who have known the worst kinds of abuse and neglect yet are still filled with joy and the love of God. How could I not be inspired by them?

I mentioned earlier that I've met thirty people born without limbs just like me. I've also met countless others who've lost limbs due to bombs in war zones, horrible accidents, or infections. I want to end this part of the book with the inspiring story of a remarkable young woman whose story is unlike any other I've ever heard.

I met Beata Jalocha, a physiotherapist from Kraków, during a 2016 speaking engagement in Poland. She had written that she hoped to meet me, so I met her and a small group of others after my speech. I could go on and on about this young woman and why she inspires me, but I think she tells her story better than I could.

I'll just say that I've recently seen photos on Beata's Facebook page of her competing in a beauty pageant, flying in a glider, skydiving in a tandem parachute, scuba diving, and soaring in a hot-air balloon with her friends.

My favorite of these photos shows her landing in the hot-air balloon's passenger basket, which ended up sideways on the ground. Beata is shown lying face up in the basket and laughing hysterically. The fact that this young woman can laugh with such joy is itself a miracle, but even more amazing is her mission to be a miracle in the lives of others after all the pain and tragedy she has experienced in the last few years.

I love that Beata, who has endured such tragedy, has it in her heart to serve as a miracle to others who have suffered and still suffer. She tells me that she knows God had a reason for her injuries and a purpose in mind for her. She is searching for answers and confident they will come. In the meantime, she isn't waiting around and feeling sorry for herself. She has a vision for the future, and she is pursuing it.

I will be honored to help her in any way I can, just as I am dedicated to helping every person I can possibly reach. My mission is to see people lead fulfilling lives here on earth and to guide them to God's home where life everlasting awaits.

I hope this book inspires you to make that your mission as well.

Be the Hands and Feet

When Life Doesn't Go as Planned

By Beata Jalocha

On Saturday, May 18, 2013, I was working as a physiotherapist in Kraków, and I left my apartment to visit a patient. This was a time when everything in my life was starting to go well. I worked at a rehabilitation center for patients with neurological problems. I had earned a permanent position after working part time as a replacement. Patients included those with spinal cord injuries.

I felt needed. These patients, in their tragedy, showed me what is important in life, and I tried to help them. My afternoons were usually spent in fitness rooms working with them. My job gave me some balance in my life. My work was very important for me, but it also challenged me physically and mentally. I liked it. I liked challenges, and each patient was a new challenge.

On that day in 2013, I had an appointment with a patient. We actually were supposed to meet at an earlier date, but we'd rescheduled at her request, which was a rare thing for me to do because I was so busy. On the day of the new appointment we were to meet at 10 a.m., but I experienced several delays on the way to her apartment. These delays proved to be quite fateful.

I could have walked to her place, which was on the same street as mine, but I decided to drive because I had plans to go somewhere else later. When I arrived, I could not remember the patient's apartment number. I had it on my cell phone, but the battery had died. I went back home to recharge the battery on my phone and sent a message to warn her that I was running thirty minutes late.

Once my phone was charged, I drove back and parked near her block. Then I reparked because there was a policewoman giving tickets to cars, and I wasn't sure if my first spot was okay. Then, after finding a better space, I parked, got out of my car, and took maybe a dozen steps.

I do not have any memories of what happened next. The police officers who first came to help me said I appeared to still be conscious. Even so, I have no memory of what happened.

My mind has wiped out the twenty-four hours after the accident. The pain likely had something to do with that. All my ribs and my spine were broken. One of my legs was completely crushed. The worst injury was my damaged spinal cord and the loss of control of the lower part of my body.

It is a miracle I'm alive. The impact from being hit by a man falling from such a height was enormous. I've been told that patients with such massive spinal injuries should be operated on as soon as possible in order to decompress the spinal cord, because irreversible paralysis can occur. I was waiting for this operation, but they first operated on my leg four days after the accident, and it was seven days before they operated on my spine. It was the worst seven days of my life.

I do not know why they did not put me in a pharmacological coma so I would not feel the pain. I suffered a lot. Less than two weeks later, my mother, who was with me all the time, had a stroke and was lying two floors below me in the same hospital. I do not have the words to tell you how difficult this was for me.

Concerned that I was not receiving proper medical attention, my former boyfriend and my sister contacted the media and made public what had happened to me. I was interviewed by reporters while I was lying in a hospital bed, barely able to breathe because almost all my ribs were broken. I felt as if there were a huge bag of stones on my chest.

Because of fractures in almost the whole spine, I had to lie still for more than a month. All I could do was look at a small area of the ceiling. I had great difficulty understanding what was being said to me during this time. I could speak only in a whisper because I had breathing difficulties. I felt as though I were slowly drowning.

When the media reported that I needed financial help to pay my medical bills and other expenses related to my injuries, people responded generously. It gave me a greater sense of security. It helped me get to where I am today, which is a long way from where I was in the first few weeks after the accident.

On the first anniversary of my accident, I wanted to feel something positive, something that would reawaken my emotions, which had been locked away all during that time. I'd become reluctant to leave the house alone, and I didn't like feeling so fearful. So I did something Nick has done: I jumped from an airplane in a tandem parachute with an instructor. I wanted to challenge myself, and it helped free me up.

Then, a few months later, I competed in the Miss Wheelchair World competition in Poland. I didn't win Miss Poland, but I was the runner-up and Miss Popularity in the competition. Winning wasn't the important thing for me; it was a motivational exercise I needed.

When you are confined to a wheelchair, you tend to withdraw. You want to hide because you feel shame and embarrassment. I had moments when I wanted to disappear, but my training as a physiotherapist and my belief system told me that I should not give up.

My health continues to be a challenge. I am paralyzed from the ribs down. I do not have control of my lower body. Otherwise, I am mostly independent. I drive a car on my own, even long distance. I am planning to live independently so as to relieve my family of that responsibility. I have to do it for them and for myself.

Despite lingering pain, I am always looking to the future, looking to meet new people and new opportunities. That is the reason I went to Nick's speaking engagement in 2016.

I wrote to the organizers, and they invited me to a private meeting with Nick and other disabled people after his speech. During the private meeting, Nick told us he plans to start a foundation to help disabled people around the world, and the first project would be in Poland.

That was very exciting to me because I have a similar dream. In Poland, there is a lack of knowledge about people with disabilities and how to treat them and integrate them into society. My dream is to create a true rehabilitation center in Poland, one dedicated to patients with spinal-cord injuries. The entire staff would have full knowledge of what is needed to help heal people with traumatic spinal injuries.

I want to help others, because as a physiotherapist who has suffered severe spinal injuries, I know it is not enough that someone teach you how to move around in a wheelchair. Someone has to show you how to live and cope with the emotional impact of being in that chair. The last three years since my accident have been a huge challenge. I am still looking for answers, still struggling to reclaim my life from that horrible, crippling event.

As difficult as it has been, you won't find me hiding in a dark corner. Instead, you'll find me parachuting, scuba diving, and flying as a newly licensed glider pilot. I do those things to prove that I am still taking risks and welcoming new experiences. Some doubted that I could pilot a glider on my own, but I proved that I could!

I told Nick that I've designed a four-stage program for treatment that includes mental training, training for sports, daily life skills, and self-esteem building. I know how hard it is to rebuild your body, mind, and spirit, but you have to fight your way back and reclaim your life and your purpose.

Nick encouraged me, and I hope one day we will work on this together. That would be wonderful. Just thinking about helping others in this way keeps me together inside. I need goals like this to be able to live with what happened to me.

The truth is, there are days when I start to doubt myself. I don't feel grief or rage, but sometimes just pain and sadness. There are days when it's really difficult for me, although I try not to burden anyone. I believe that nothing happens without a reason and that Someone up there has a plan for me that I have to accomplish. I also believe in people and that the good comes back to you.

Part III

FINISH WELL

11

MY FATHER—A MODEL FOR LIFE

My father often said that my career as the hands and feet of Jesus was foreshadowed when I was just eighteen months old. My parents took me to a church camp in Virginia during our first visit to the United States in 1984. It was summer, very hot and humid, and they took me for a ride in a stroller to try to cool off in the evening.

An elder with the church-camp group met us on the path. He leaned down and said something to me, but I was having a rare moment of shyness. Instead of turning on my toddler charm, I turned away from him. Maybe I was cranky because of the heat. Maybe I didn't feel like engaging with another stranger or I just needed a break. I wasn't quite two years old, or I'd blame the terrible twos.

Despite my shunning, the elder later called my parents and asked if he could talk about me in his sermon to the entire camp at that night's service. My parents agreed, although they had no idea what he was planning to say. As it turned out, his sermon was titled "No Place to Hide," and it was based on 2 Corinthians 5:10: "For we must all appear before the judgment seat of Christ, so that each one may receive what is due us for what he has done in the body, whether good or evil."

The elder talked about my shy response to him. He compared my turning away to what will happen on the Day of Judgment, when people who haven't been faithful to God will hide their faces from Him. He quoted Revelation 6:16: "They called to the mountains and the rocks, 'Fall on us and hide us from the face of him who sits on the throne and from the wrath of the Lamb!'" (NIV).

My parents said the elder also referred to Psalm 139:7: "Where shall I go from your Spirit? Or where shall I flee from your presence?"

I guess my father's point was that at a very young age I was already serving as a lesson to other Christians in a sermon, although frankly I think the elder was stretching the point a bit. Turning my head from a stranger wasn't exactly like turning away from God on the Day of Judgment, but I will defer to Dad on this one because he is, after all, my role model for a devoted Christian man.

I often think of Proverbs 13:20 when I think of my dad: "Whoever walks with the wise becomes wise." My father, Boris Vujicic, now walks with God in heaven, although we still feel his presence and his wonderful spirit every moment of every day. He departed on Sunday, May 14, 2017. He had been diagnosed with terminal cancer about a year and a half before that, shortly after completing the book he wrote called *Raising the Perfectly Imperfect Child*. Yes, that would be me. My father also assisted me with this book, and of course, he and my mother have been sources of strength, support, and inspiration my entire life.

Just as I may serve as a role model for many other perfectly imperfect Christians, my father served as mine. I feel that way not only because he had such strong faith in God but because of the way he lived each and every day. He always believed the best way to attract nonbelievers to Jesus was to be a living example of Christian values. He was a faithful, patient, humble, loving, and disciplined soldier of Christ.

Dad was always a pillar of strength and an example of courage. That was especially true after he received the second biggest shock of his life. (I was his first big shock, of course.) In his book, my father wrote about his reliance on God's strength after my birth. There had been no indication I would arrive without limbs. He and my mum at first struggled to understand our heavenly Father's plan and purpose for their unusual first child.

The second major shock in my father's life also required his asking God for strength. It occurred shortly after his book was submitted to the publisher in 2015. He was diagnosed with stage IV cholangiocarcinoma cancer and told he had only four to eight weeks to live.

My father had never had serious health issues, so this was stunning news. Two years before his brother Milos had been diagnosed with pancreatic cancer, and he died sixteen weeks later. Dad knew how agonizing this kind of cancer could be, and he prayed for strength and grace. He consulted other doctors, and they weren't sure where his cancer originated, because it was found in his pancreas, liver, and lungs. Most thought he'd live only a month or two if he didn't begin chemotherapy, but even then, they thought he had only a year at the most.

Dad amazed us all with his strength and resilience. He lived well beyond the short time his doctors gave him in their initial diagnosis. He went for a long time without experiencing much pain, which is truly a miracle since he opted out of the standard treatments after only a couple of weeks.

STAYING IN FAITH

My father often said that one of the high points of his life was having grandchildren, and just as he was beginning to enjoy them, he entered this valley of suffering and fear, one of the lowest of his life. He handled this unexpected ordeal with as much grace and dignity as I've ever witnessed in someone facing death.

He credited his positive attitude to his lifelong Christian beliefs. He said the cancer would one day deplete his strength and defeat his body, but it would never rob him of either his faith or the peace he derived from knowing that his Father in heaven and life everlasting awaited him.

Living as a Christian role model every day in today's world is challenging enough when you are healthy and untroubled. Staying in faith and living with grace when your body is battling cancer is much more difficult. Yet from the very beginning, Dad drew upon his spiritual beliefs. He put his faith in action, inspiring all of us and teaching us through his example.

My father first noticed in the summer of 2015 that he was lacking energy while he was playing tennis. He also began taking naps, sometimes twice a day, which was highly unusual for him. The only other physical difference was that when he had his usual glass of wine with dinner, it upset his stomach and made him feel a little sick. Around this same time, some other aunts and uncles were having health issues, so my father agreed to go in for a checkup and a colonoscopy. The blood tests all came back fine, although he experienced bloating and cramping.

When Dad continued to have pain in his stomach, my mum scheduled another appointment. This resulted in another round of blood tests that showed his liver function levels were a little high. The doctor ordered an ultrasound and found a lump on his liver. An MRI found three tumors on the liver and one on the pancreas. There also appeared to be spots on his lungs, though my father had never been a smoker.

When Milos had been diagnosed and told by his doctors he had only about sixteen weeks to live even with chemotherapy, my uncle went along with their advice. He was very sick during his treatments and died four months after his diagnosis.

All this was on our minds when Dad received his diagnosis.

His doctors said Dad might have only a month or two with us unless he did chemotherapy, which might buy him another six months or so. My father was very reluctant to do it because of what had happened to his brother.

When there is a medical crisis in a family these days, everyone tends to rush to the Internet to search for some answers. In our case, my mother, sister, and sister-in-law are nurses, and my brother, Aaron, was a biology and physics major. They brought considerable expertise and experience to the table. It is important to know what questions to ask your doctors and what sources are reliable on the Internet, so their depth of knowledge was very helpful.

My mother and sister had witnessed the devastating impact of standard chemotherapy treatments on patients. They knew that many in the medical community consider chemotherapy to be a very aggressive option because of the potential damage done to a body's organs and immune system.

The trend now is to use drugs and protocols that specifically target and destroy cancer cells or to follow a treatment plan that boosts the body's natural defenses to attack the cancer. Some advocate so-called natural or alternative treatments such as juices made from raw vegetables and fruits, vitamins and other supplements, or a combination of the two.

Through family and friends, we had connections to doctors around the world. While on a speaking engagement for the Lifeline Humanitarian Organization that helps the neediest people in my family's native country of Serbia, I'd gotten to know Alexander and Katherine Karadordevic, the crowned prince and princess. They were very helpful in recommending and linking us to medical experts.

My family sought out several cancer specialists to get their opinions. There are so many different opinions and different treatments, standard and experimental, that it boggles the mind. You hear of some people who manage to live years beyond their doctor's estimates, while others succumb within a matter of days and weeks.

Although there was some disagreement on whether the cancer had originated in his liver or his pancreas, our medical advisors agreed it was a very aggressive cancer and that Dad's time was limited. Our challenge was to find the best treatment that would allow a quality of life without pain and suffering.

Eventually we found a cancer specialist in Los Angeles who used a modified chemotherapy approach that he said would be less intense than standard protocols. It was supposed to be easier on patients and have fewer harsh side effects, such as intense pain, nausea, and vomiting. This doctor promised his alternative methods would have fewer ill effects on Dad's overall health.

HAUNTING DREAMS

Avoiding pain is always a good option, and in our case, it was a priority. My father and I shared a very low tolerance for pain and sickness. Dad took two weeks to consider his treatment options. Needless to say, he prayed on it, and we prayed for him as well. Despite his concern about side effects, he agreed to try chemotherapy.

Unfortunately, his fears about getting sick from the treatments were quickly realized. Every patient reacts differently, so maybe the doctor's promises were based on more positive results with others. Dad did two treatments in two weeks. He didn't have any extreme side effects after the first treatment, but he became violently ill after the second. He suffered intense nausea, vomiting, and diarrhea. He couldn't eat and could hardly drink.

My mum and sister wanted to take him to an emergency room, but Dad refused. He thought they'd want him to stay overnight, and he preferred to be at home with family. I was called in to convince him to go to the ER. Their big concern was that Dad was dehydrated, which can lead to kidney failure. I promised him that we would not leave him at the hospital unless there was something terribly wrong.

My mum drove him to the hospital around 10 p.m. on a Sunday. The waiting room was packed. My mother told them Dad was having a bad response to chemotherapy, but that didn't seem to make any difference to the people in charge. As they waited and waited, he grew pale. He said he felt very weak. Mum was worried that his kidneys were failing.

AN ANGEL OF MERCY

Just as my mother was beginning to panic, a nurse appeared and introduced herself as a family friend. She is a neighbor of my cousin who lives near us in California. She had recognized my parents because she'd seen them at a Fourth of July party at my cousin's house that summer. My parents didn't recognize her, but they were grateful when she offered to assist them.

She took them into the ER, gave my father an IV to ease his dehydration, and waited with them until a doctor came in. She then introduced my parents as friends to the ER doctor and asked that he'd take good care of him. Having an advocate in the room made a huge difference. The doctor took very good care of my father, and Dad felt better once his dehydration was addressed. They gave him two liters of fluids.

My father decided that night he would not continue with chemotherapy. I've always teased him about being cautious. He's long warned me about my tendency to take risks. It was ironic, then, that my father chose the less cautious path with this major decision.

He was willing to trade any extra time the chemotherapy might bring him for a better quality of life during the time he had left with us. We didn't blame him at all. If he only had a few weeks or months left, he didn't want to be so sick he couldn't be with his loved ones. Because of his faith, Dad wasn't the least bit afraid of dying. He was quite open and frank about that.

After this experience, Dad followed a juicing regimen of green juices and kale that my sister created for him based on her research into natural cancer treatments designed to regenerate his liver and boost his immune system. A few of his tumors were quite large, but Dad frequently said, "Someone with these issues shouldn't feel as good as I feel."

MAKING THE MOST OF OUR TIME

Once he quit chemotherapy and felt better, he called us together for a family breakfast. He read from the Bible and then talked about the importance of staying close to God and His Word. He also asked for our forgiveness for anything he might have done to hurt or offend us. Dad was beginning the process of saying goodbye to his earthly life. That family gathering was the first of many in which we talked about our faith, our love for each other, and the many blessings we'd shared.

Some people facing death don't want to talk about it; others go into the victim role. My father sought to prepare his family and himself by sharing his faith and love. Now, I'm sure he had his private moments of grief and despair. I saw his eyes grow moist while playing with his grandsons.

We did not hide from our grief either, but we wanted to make the most of our remaining days with him. There were family cookouts, prayer sessions, and outings. My parents even went on a three-day cruise, which was a great gift and a chance to relax after so much stress.

Facing the end of life does make a person reflective, of course. My father naturally had concerns about missing out on the important events every parent looks forward to. My sister, Michelle, had always talked about having Dad walk her down the aisle when she married one day. Sadly, he never had the opportunity.

Dad was grateful for the time he spent with our sons, Kiyoshi and Dejan, our second child who was born just three weeks before Dad was diagnosed. My father wanted his grandchildren to know him and to remember him, and we will make certain of that.

Shortly after Dad's diagnosis, we gathered for some family photos, and

Dad teared up during the session with the photographer. When someone said we were taking the photos for him, my father laughed sadly and said, "I will be gone, so they will be for you, not for me."

THE POWER OF HOPE

We all chose to pray for the best outcome instead of falling into grief and despair. We prayed for God's guidance and wisdom. We prayed that His plan was for my father to continue on earth as an example for other Christians facing crises.

When someone you love is diagnosed with a life-threatening illness, everything else in your life loses significance. Your job, not to mention all your most pressing concerns and plans, fade out of your consciousness. All I could think about was my father and how much he meant to me and our family.

My dad, in typical fashion, focused on his family instead of himself. The man facing death consoled us. One day, he called me over to his house to help put his affairs in order so my mother wouldn't have to worry when he was gone. Dad didn't want us dwelling on his illness. He urged us to make the most of whatever time was left.

Challenges like this remind us that every day is a gift and that, after our faith in God, our relationships are our biggest treasures. We expressed gratitude for the fact that, for the first time in a decade, all our immediate family members, as well as many aunts, uncles, and cousins, were living on the same continent and in the same state so we could spend time with my father.

My brother, Aaron, and his wife and my sister, Michelle, had all followed my parents to California, where I have lived for many years. We were able to rally around Dad, along with aunts, uncles, and cousins. That would not have been possible when we were all scattered about on different continents.

I can't imagine how hard it would have been on the family if my brother and his wife and Michelle hadn't been close by. We often prayed together during this period, and we made sure we thanked God that we had each other to lean on during such a difficult time.

We took every opportunity to celebrate as a family after my father's diagnosis. He inspired us by hanging in there and proving his doctors initial estimates wrong. Kanae and I had always loved watching Dad play with Kiyoshi, and we were ever more grateful he was here for the birth of our second child, held him, and loved him.

For my father, it was bittersweet. He was so glad to have grandchildren, but it saddened him to think he wouldn't watch them grow into adults.

He often admitted to me, after I married, that when I was younger he didn't think I would ever find a wife and have children. He felt that God sent Kanae and my sons. My father liked to hold our boys and sing Serbian folk songs to them. He would sometimes have tears flowing as he sang, but he sang nonetheless.

God allows us to go through valleys so He can guide us through them, and then we can share our testimony of praying for and receiving His strength. I am thankful for the ups and downs. I really am. Yes, it is difficult to summon gratitude when your world seems to be crashing down around you, especially when someone you love is hurting. Still, there is always something you can be thankful for.

For all the tears and grieving over my father's cancer and his passing, I am grateful to have witnessed the strength of his faith in such a trying time. My mum and dad were closer than they've ever been. My father had never shown so much peace. Our family has always been close, but we came together like never before. Our love overflowed.

God's glory was revealed in all this, and that's the bottom line. We knew that if Dad lost his battle with cancer, he would go home to His heavenly Father. His passing was God's will. Our loss was God's gain.

A PARTING GIFT

While writing his book about parenting me, *Raising the Perfectly Imperfect Child,* Dad was struck by the fact that God didn't give him and Mum the vision to see how my life would unfold because He was testing their faith under fire to make them stronger Christians. God turned what had seemed like a great tragedy—a severely disabled child—into a blessing, not just for my parents, but for many others. The "imperfect" child turned out to be perfectly suited to God's plan.

"God brought a victory that I couldn't see in the beginning, at Nick's birth, so I learned to trust in His plan," my father said. "I was thinking of that when I received my diagnosis of stage IV cancer. At first it was another big shock, another slap in the face. I felt like Job, initially, whose faith was tested by the loss of family members and his livestock. In the story of Job, at first he is affected because of the suffering of those around him, but then God tests him again by bringing suffering directly to him. So it was the same with me. Instead of me worrying about Nick and his challenges, I was the one faced with a major physical challenge. God was testing me directly, just as he had Job."

Dad said that while he was working on his book and reading through its lessons, he found peace with the cancer diagnosis and surrendered the outcome to God. "I felt with the completion of the book, in some aspects my race had been run and my purpose accomplished, so I could accept this new challenge and make the most of the time remaining with my family," he said.

When we first learned of Dad's diagnosis, we didn't know if he'd be healthy enough or even with us when his book was published. It was another great blessing to share that experience with him. His book taught me so much about what a great man of faith my father has always been.

I attended several of Dad's book signings. I'm grateful that he heard from readers who appreciated the book and his guidance. My father was a private person, so it was a stretch for him to write about his feelings and experiences and even more of a stretch to talk about them in interviews and at book signings. He was willing to put himself out there, because he thought other parents and children would benefit. He felt that God created me for a purpose, and part of that plan was to give hope and encouragement to others with disabilities.

My father was deeply touched by the positive responses of his readers. I get a lot of rewarding feedback from my audiences, so I think it's really cool that Dad heard from so many grateful people too.

For me, being a Christian is about having a positive impact on the lives of others and guiding them toward everlasting life. My father deserves credit for any good I do on earth. I've told him there will be a long line in heaven of those who want to thank him. The book signings we've done together are a little sample of that, a little taste of heaven for him.

As I came to know him, man to man, I had a clearer view of his quiet strength, giving heart, and gift for empathy with others. My father was quieter than me, but he is a true Christian role model without a doubt. This is my father's legacy as a devoted Christian, the fruit of his living as such a powerful example of obedience and trust in God. It will endure through me and hopefully through my sons too.

A MODEL OF GRACE

We would not have blamed my father if he'd retreated from view to prepare for his journey to everlasting life. The prospect of dying within a short time can drive anyone to despair. Once again, though, Dad displayed grace and strength under pressure.

We deal with many challenges throughout our days by saying, "Well, this isn't a life-threatening situation." Except when you are confronted with what is truly just that. Then your perspective shifts in a hurry. Facing death brought the reality of heaven and his belief in God into sharper focus, Dad said. When diagnosed with stage IV cancer, death, too, becomes a greater reality.

When we are young, we tend to take it for granted that our parents will always be around. As we get older, we see them age, and the reality sets in that our time together is limited. Yet we don't expect to lose our parents in their early sixties when so many live into their seventies and eighties. In truth, we are never ready to let them go.

My father and I had many heart-to-heart talks after his diagnosis. He reminded me that, as Christians, we know there will be a second coming of Christ and all the faithful will be called into heaven. We believe there is life after death. Dad said that knowledge sustained him, and it should sustain us through this trial. Eventually we will all be together in heaven, and that is our hope and our comfort. It all comes down to faith. My father said he can't imagine that we cease to exist after we leave our earthly bodies behind.

The question he had to confront was, "Am I ready to face God?" He wanted to make sure he was prepared spiritually. Dad recalled that when his mother was dying at age seventy-seven, she said the only thing she would miss was seeing her grandchildren grow up, and it was the same for my father. Beyond that, he felt ready to go to God.

Dad said we should all keep in mind that heaven is real and be grateful that he was well prepared for eternal life in God's grace. I understood that and believe it with all my heart, but of course we want our parents to always be there for every event in the lives of our children.

A PARENT'S BURDEN

We often used to tease Dad for stressing out about things. Now I'll find myself staring at the mirror, wondering how I became so stressed out. My father stares back at me. I find myself fretting just as he did over family matters and finances and all the things that grown-ups have to deal with. We were different in many ways, yet more and more I notice the similarities. I credit my mum and dad for passing their best characteristics to me, especially their faith and determination.

I've come to understand that my father's mission was to fulfill God's plan for him and to help his children go further than he could ever go. He came from a very poor immigrant background. I only recently discovered that my father was bullied by a classroom teacher because he was one of the few Christians in his school. His own father had been a pacifist in Serbia, and family members were bullied and shunned because they refused to bear arms in the military.

My father talked more about his life once his death seemed nearer. I can see that I have risen higher on my father's shoulders. God propelled me forward as a Christian role model, but my purpose was nourished by the sacrifices, the wisdom, and the lessons learned from my mother and father. Dad worked three jobs for many years while also volunteering to plant churches, counseling individuals, and raising three children.

Since becoming a father myself, I've often wondered, *How on earth did my parents raise a child with no arms or legs?* Our two able-bodied sons are a challenge enough. More than once I've had to pray for more of God's strength so I can be as good a father as my dad.

The one thing my father and I seriously clashed over was my belief that I could visit other churches without tainting or corrupting my faith. His own parents had to practice their faith secretly, so my father came from a tradition in which people were intensely loyal to their churches and denominations. He wanted his children to attend his church as a family, even when we became adults. Dad always said, "If this church is not good enough for my kids, why is it good enough for me?"

The problem grew when I reached my twenties and began speaking far and wide to many different denominations. I wanted to share my testimony around the world as a soldier of Christ; Dad wanted me to pursue a career in accounting and business management. He thought I was more suited to an office job than traveling the globe.

My father also feared I had led a fairly sheltered life within our family's church. He was afraid I would be influenced more by other churches than they would be influenced by me. I listened to his concerns, but I felt called and convicted.

At the time, I could only pray to God that He would take care of my parents' hearts. I felt a calling to something they didn't want me to do. We butted heads over different visions of my future. Eventually, my father came to see that I could go out into the world without losing focus on my faith.

I did my best to honor my parents. I'm grateful I finished my accounting and financial planning degrees because I've benefited in many ways from what I learned. I am thankful I followed God's call to inspire hope and plant faith in people around the world. My Father in heaven created me for this work, and my father on earth has been my inspirational role model.

Through his health crisis and throughout his life, my father's faith in God kept him anchored. It was a blessing to see his faith in action. His hope elevated him above the challenges and circumstances of his cancer. His gratitude reached new heights. He and my mum felt blessed for the time they had together.

When my father was still feeling strong enough to write, I asked him to offer you some parting advice. I wasn't sure he would want to do it—he was so humble—but I am glad that he did. Here it is, just as he wrote it.

Be the Hands and Feet

Reflections of a Father

By Boris Vujicic

Diseases and illnesses can take your health and even your life, but they can't take your peace and they can't take your faith.

When faced with stage IV cancer, you continue in the same faith and conviction. You pray. You trust God. That has been my approach.

The Bible says our days are numbered and that nothing happens without His knowledge; even a sparrow does not fall. In the end, that gives me peace. It doesn't matter whether I take chemotherapy or drink juices or do anything else. I believe we cannot change or add a day to our lives unless God has predetermined it.

Nothing causes God to change His mind. He has already taken everything into account. A lot of people struggle to understand this. Some argue that God does change His mind. They cite Scripture in which Isaiah the prophet was sent to King Hezekiah and told him to set his life in order because he was going to die. The righteous king was sad and prayed to God.

The interesting part is that God told Isaiah to go back to Hezekiah and tell him He had extended his life for another fifteen years. Some say God changed His mind; however, in my opinion, God knows the future, and so, from the beginning, He had accounted for this additional fifteen years. It was predetermined how long this king would live.

I believe if God has determined me to be saved, I will be saved. Some take that attitude because they say God has preordained our lives will end with our going to either heaven or hell, but I believe that is misinterpreting free choice. God gives it to us, but He knows what our choices will be and He can forecast what will happen. God is perfect, and He is always right.

The doctor originally said I might live two to six months, and now, as I write this, it's been thirteen months. It could be another year or another ten years. I basically trust my life to God's ancient wisdom. I believe I will not die one day before or one day after the time He has allocated to me, and I'm at peace with that.

I think that Jesus felt the same thing while on earth. He knew that God had set His time to die. When enemies threatened to throw Jesus off a cliff, it was not yet time to die. But when that time came, Jesus said, "This is it."

He was God in the flesh and recognized that fact. I believe God has given me an increase, for which I am very grateful, and I remain hopeful. A lady in our church also was given six months to live with cancer, and she is still going strong eleven years later. She has given me encouragement, which is always good to hear.

My confidence is in God, and I know that His will, not mine, will be done. I have tried to live a good Christian existence. But the Bible says that God will take a righteous person home to spare that individual from suffering and a calamity that awaits.

We don't know what lies ahead, so we can't fathom that death might be a blessing. God's eye sees all. If God determines that my time has come, then so be it. He knows what is coming, and He knows what I can and can't bear.

It is comforting to know that my family is ready to accept whatever God decides. When Nick was just a child, he had a lot of questions about dying and life after death. I recall three questions he asked me one day.

1. What will heaven be like?
2. Would he have arms and legs in heaven?
3. Would we recognize each other and live as a family in heaven?

I may have the answer to question number one sooner than I'd thought. I certainly hope I have a long, long time to ponder the other two. What makes me happy about those questions, though, is the fact that, at a young age, my son assumed we would all be together in heaven one day. I could not imagine a heaven without my family.

The extension of my life so far is maybe a time for us to fully accept and be thankful for our shared faith and Christian beliefs. As of this writing, I still have a good quality of life, considering everything, and I am thankful to God for every minute.

I am thankful I saw Dejan's first birthday and that I have seen him walk and love his brother, Kiyoshi, too. I appreciate each day more for the opportunity to be with them, for the sunshine I see, for the mountains I see, for the time I am in church and with my loved ones. I reflect often on each moment, thinking, *They said I wasn't supposed to be here, so this is a bonus.*

I've come to appreciate life in many more aspects than I ever did before. I'm not held to possessions. For one thing, I was looking forward to retirement and to enjoying traveling more. We had planned a trip to Serbia, but I didn't get to do it. I would have loved to have seen more of the world, but it is not that crucial.

As a normal person, you can enjoy your family, food and drink, and peace of mind. Really, that is the most you can hope for in life. It would be nice to live another ten or fifteen years and see more of my grandkids growing up. That would be a nice blessing, but it is not as important as being saved and having faith in God.

Because of my faith, I don't feel a devastating loss in my diagnosis, but maybe I'm an odd person. I just want to know that Dushka will be fine. We share things with each other. She does all the finance. She does all the banking, and I have no idea about all that. I would be lost without her paying the bills. Thank God, she won't be lost without me. Most of the time, I don't know what she is doing with the money. I tell her I trust her until the sheriff comes in the door and says we have to get out.

I am most grateful our children have the same faith in God and the same hope, so I know all of them will one day be with Him too. All of them will have futures beyond this life, and that is a great assurance for me. I am comforted also to know that my children are all well established. Nick, with his disability, was a major concern early in his life, but he has done incredibly well. I can go with comfort and peace knowing that Nick, Aaron, and Michelle will all continue to do well.

When you are looking at the reality of being with God after you die, He becomes so much more real. I might not actually miss what is here, because I will enjoy the other aspects of the afterlife. I don't know if I'll be aware of what goes on here after I've moved on. I don't know how much awareness we have. God knows. The angels are also aware.

I have some indication there is a possibility I may know what is going on, because there is a passage in Revelation that says those who have passed away asked God how long He would let evil continue on earth before He brings judgment and restoration. That seems to at least hint that those in heaven are aware of life here.

I am grateful also that I was able to complete my book about raising Nick. Going to book signings has strengthened my family and our faith. People all around the world know Nick, and since he asked for prayers for me on Facebook, many are praying for me.

With everybody praying, I believe God is answering and responding. In the Bible, James says that if anyone among us is sick, all the elders should pray, and God will heal that person. I took that literally and put it into practice, asking the elders in my church to pray for me and do the anointing.

All the vitamin supplements and juicing are well and good, but above all, my continued good health is due to God. My life is in His hands, and I believe that it's God's answer to the prayers. This is all part of his calculated and predetermined time for me. That is encouraging to know for everyone and others in our church. Many prayed for me, saying they needed to keep me around. It has been encouraging that many have come to me and said their faith has been strengthened by seeing me handle this situation with confidence and calm.

I feel their prayers for me have been answered, and it has helped them in their faith. I understand this is not so much about what it means to me and more about building the faith of those around me. In that way, I've remained a soldier in God's army by serving as an example for other Christians. As I noted earlier, cancer and other illnesses can take your life, but they cannot take your peace, and they cannot take your faith.

12

NO MATTER WHAT COMES

After my father's cancer diagnosis in the fall of 2015, we had many serious family discussions. One of the concerns was that our family members seemed to be susceptible to cancers. My father's brother had died of pancreatic cancer. Other relatives had died of colon cancer. Naturally, we worried that, based on this history, some form of the disease might strike again in our family.

Kanae had been urging me to get a checkup every year. I understood she was looking out for me. She knows I avoid doctors and hospitals as much as possible. I've spent so much of my life being probed and picked at by physicians that I have to be seriously ill to go in voluntarily.

Doctors aren't thrilled to see me either. Medical procedures considered to be routine for most people become more complicated for me because of my unique body. A simple thing like taking blood pressure or a blood sample is a challenge when a nurse can't tap into the major veins in arms or legs.

I resisted checkups also because we'd been to the emergency room with

Kiyoshi several times because of his mysterious pains. I was burned out on hospital waiting rooms and the whole medical environment.

Still, there was something else nagging me. I hadn't told Kanae or anyone else that a few weeks before learning of my father's cancer diagnosis, I experienced pain spasms similar to Kiyoshi's. They lasted only a few seconds and they were intermittent, only a couple of times a week.

Sorry if that is too much information, but there isn't any way to write around this sort of thing. Simply put, I had pain while peeing. I might have ignored it, since it was just a sporadic thing, but after my father's diagnosis, I felt a responsibility to my family to have a checkup.

The Bible tells us that when Hezekiah became ill and faced death, the prophet Isaiah said, "This is what the LORD says: Put your house in order, because you are going to die; you will not recover" (2 Kings 20:1, NIV).

At that point, I was contemplating not my own death but my father's stage IV cancer, and our battle with Kiyoshi's mysterious pain had me feeling vulnerable. I was inspired by the way my dad surrendered his fear to God and put his life in His hands. When I told him how much I admired his serenity and acceptance, my father reminded me of Matthew 6:27: "And which of you by being anxious can add a single hour to his span of life?"

Instead of being upset, feeling sorry for himself, or grieving, Dad devoted all his energy to putting his affairs in order so that my mum wouldn't have to deal with any major issues after his passing.

I admired my father for that. I felt like I wasn't even in the same league. I told myself I was younger. My family was younger. I had at least half my life ahead of me. My dad was in his sixties. I was just into my thirties.

He was spiritually mature. I wasn't there yet. That is a humbling realization for someone who travels the world to inspire others with his faith. I embrace that humility. That must be God's plan, because He keeps providing me with humbling experiences.

I was about to embark on one of the biggest ever.

A WALK THROUGH THE VALLEY

When I went for the checkup, my doctor ordered an MRI and colonoscopy. Normally these are outpatient procedures, but not for me. Because they cannot readily monitor my blood pressure or insert an IV to give me fluids, the doctors have to use my jugular vein. It is not a pleasant thought or experience, trust me.

Putting me asleep during an operation is another challenge. The usual formulas for anesthesia don't apply for my special body. The same amount used on an average person could easily knock out ol' Nick permanently.

And I was a new patient for this doctor, so he had to do a lot of research. After studying his options, he suggested doing a virtual colonoscopy instead of the usual method. Honestly, I broke out laughing when he said that. I had visions of him wearing a virtual reality headset as if he were playing a video game in my digestive system.

"Not quite," he said, but this high-tech approach does not require putting me under with anesthesia. Instead, they use a CAT scan, X-rays, and computers to produce 3-D images of my digestive tract.

A SENSITIVITY ISSUE

I am always glad to go with the least invasive available procedure. The bad news was that the virtual version of a colonoscopy is painful because you aren't under anesthesia, and it is more expensive. But since I'm so wary of anesthesia, I agreed to do the virtual colonoscopy, though I had serious reservations about the potential for pain.

I convinced myself they would have to give me some sort of painkiller, even if it was just a pill. You see, I have a long and painful history with pain, but I have a very good semi-scientific theory that explains my severe wimpiness when it comes to all things involving doctors, hospitals, and especially needles.

I believe my nerve endings are hypersensitive or hyperactive or just hyper. Some people are thin-skinned; I'm short-skinned. I have half the amount of skin most people have, so I think that plays a part. I seem to be ten times more sensitive to touch. If there is a bug on my body, I know it right away, and that can be a little maddening when you don't have arms and hands to slap at them.

I've written before about the nightmarish European road trip when we left a window open in my hotel room and I was swarmed by Transylvanian mosquitos that covered my body in bites because I couldn't fight them off. The itching from the vampire bugs nearly drove me mad.

Long before that horrible experience, I had an even creepier boyhood experience in Australia when I wondered if I was losing my mind. I was about thirteen years old when I felt invisible things crawling on my face, hair, chest, and shoulders.

I looked in the mirror, but I couldn't see anything. But I had no doubt something was crawling in my hair. The sensation made my face twitch and my head itch. I'd run to the mirror and examine the twitching and itching areas, but I could not see anything. The creepy crawly feeling would stop for a while and then begin again. The sensation was very real despite the lack of visible evidence. I begged my mum to look several times. She couldn't find anything either. So I'd plead for her to scratch my head to give me relief.

I really thought I was losing it. My mum did too. One day when I felt the crawlies on my cheek, I ran to a magnifying mirror and turned on a bright light. By the time I was all set up to see the cause of it, the sensation stopped. I decided to wait and see if the feeling returned.

I can be patient when I'm on the hunt. I can watch a fishing line for hours. So I applied my fisherman's patience to stalking the source of my itchiness. I waited and watched for maybe twenty minutes before I felt it again.

I looked into the mirror under the bright light, and this time I saw a tiny dot moving across my cheek. I blinked to clear my eyes and looked again. It was still there.

Validation!

I'm not crazy!

My facial tick, or whatever it was, appeared to be smaller than the period at the end of this sentence. But it was definitely some sort of creepy crawly moving slowly across my face. I yelled for my mum, and she came to have a look. It took her a second to spot it, but she saw it too.

"Oh, Nick, you have nits," she said sadly.

"Nits?"

Me? Nit? Nick?

"What's a nit?"

"Head lice, son."

My mom is a medical professional, so there was no doubting her diagnosis. She knew how to treat and get rid of head lice, but she was not happy about the discovery, because if one person in a family gets them, they can be spread to everyone. All family members would have to be checked and treated if they had nits too.

Mum may have been appalled, but I was delighted I finally knew what was bugging me. I was probably happier about having nits than anyone has ever been. I'll take the lice, and thank you, Lord, for letting me know I'm just buggy and not bonkers.

My mum bought the head-lice treatment at our pharmacy, but first we had to figure out where they were coming from. The answer wasn't hard to find, but it was more than a little gross. We traced the nits to my bedroom.

We discovered the sneaky bugs were coming in through the window screen. They had taken up residence in a vacated bird's nest under the eaves of the roof. We removed the bird's nest to be rid of the source. My mum then gave me the shampoo-and-soap treatments to debug her boy, marking the end of my creepy crawly facial feelings.

MEDICAL MISADVENTURE

Not many people can feel such teeny creatures creeping on them. After this incident, we all agreed I have hypersensitive skin. This high level of sensitivity unfortunately also sends me through the roof if anyone in a white coat approaches me with a hypodermic needle.

Many people fear needles. Nobody likes to receive an injection. I've been known to pass out at the mere mention of a medical shot. Needless to say, I was a wreck as the day approached. I was on edge and then I nearly went over the edge because of a mix-up in the schedule. You have to take a colon cleanser the night before a colonoscopy. If you've had this procedure, you know how awful it is. Even if you've never been through it, you can probably imagine how truly wretched this experience is.

The stuff tastes like chalk dust mixed with buttermilk, and the effects of drinking the putrid concoction make even the proudest person humble in a hurry.

I did my duty the night before, and I survived the desired but undesirable results. I was feeling like a good soldier the next morning. I manned up and did what was required. My colonoscopy appointment was at 11 a.m. I wanted to make sure I had the right address, so I called my doctor's office to confirm everything a couple of hours before the appointment.

I freaked out when the receptionist said she had no record of an appointment for me that day! I'd been up half the night doing my cleanse and now she was telling me I didn't have an appointment?

"I cleansed, so I'm coming in anyway," I told her.

They might not have been ready for me, but I was ready for them.

The doctor's assistant said they'd try to find a way to get me in for the virtual colonoscopy, but there was some concern that I'd used the wrong cleansing potion for the procedure. After some debate, they decided a cleanse was a cleanse.

I was cleared to go. What a relief! I did not want to have to drink another drop of that dreadful potion. For the first time in my life, I was happy to see my doctor. I was obviously delusional. It won't happen again.

SERIOUS THREAT

When they told me the virtual colonoscopy would be painful, I assumed they were talking about "virtual pain," not real pain. I was wrong. The pain was intense. Again, this may belong under the "too much information" heading, but they basically fill you up with air to get the X-rays. I felt like a human party balloon, and this was not a fun party.

I was relieved when it was over, but not for long. During the procedure they found the source of the pain I'd been experiencing, and it posed a serious threat. There was a tumor in my bladder, a sizable mass, hanging from a stem attached to the upper bladder wall. This was very rare, and that made it all the scarier.

It also was a shocker. The doctor said they had to shave out the whole tumor to determine if it was cancerous or benign. This meant another operation and more challenges for my unusual body. This time they put me under with anesthesia administered with a mask. They also found a vein in my foot for the IV.

We were all worried, of course. I was concerned for my parents, who were already dealing with Dad's life-threatening cancer. And I was worried for Kanae, too, because she had enough on her plate caring for our young sons.

I was grateful we are a prayerful family of strong faith. We pray daily to thank God for His blessings, so we do not feel like fair-weather Christians when challenging times hit. The lines are already open and waiting for our calls, as the infomercials say.

Many prayers were said by my wife, my parents and siblings, other relatives, friends, and me too. As it turned out, we needed every prayer that went out and maybe a few more. My surgery was performed at 9 a.m. near my home in California. After they cleared me to go home, I thought the worst was over.

We wouldn't get the results of the biopsy for several days, so all I could do was recover and wait. That first night at home, I noticed some blood in my urine and pain when I peed, but my doctor said that was to be expected. Our concern grew when the pain intensified and there were visible clots. They didn't hurt as bad as kidney stones, but I was really hurting.

I might have yelped a few times. Okay, I screamed like a banshee. The nurses in the family—my mum and my sister, Michelle—were called for a consultation, and they issued a prompt ruling: "Get to the emergency room now!"

BACK TO THE ER

I had been drinking water, as ordered, but there was bleeding in my bladder, and the clots were building up, causing my bladder to expand. You get the picture. My poor body was turning into a water balloon and was about to burst.

We were rescued from a long wait in the emergency room by a family friend, the same nurse who had helped my father get quick attention during his visit to the ER. She escorted me to a doctor who checked me out right away. They put in a catheter to relieve the pressure and pain. Then they moved me into a room for the night so they could monitor the bleeding.

Late that night, Michelle came to check on me. She had once volunteered as a nurse on the *Africa Mercy,* the largest private hospital ship in the world, so she has seen it all. When Michelle checked my catheter bag, she freaked out. It was full of very red blood. That was not a good sign.

Michelle called my doctor, who had gone home. She demanded he come back to the hospital immediately. He protested, saying some blood was to be expected. Michelle went all-out on my behalf and told him she knew what a normal catheter bag looked like, and this was not normal.

You don't mess with Michelle when she turns into a supernurse. My doctor returned to the hospital and saw that she was right. He sent me in for emergency surgery. Sixteen hours after my initial surgery, I was back on the table.

My blood pressure was dropping to dangerous levels. My pain was off the charts. I was screaming so loud my face was bright red. The anesthesiologist was afraid I'd pass out. He put an IV in my neck. My neck!

Kanae, Michelle, and my parents were there, but they had to leave the room because of my tormented cries. I've never screamed like that in my life. I've never felt so close to death, and I definitely was not feeling ready for it.

Yes, I am a Christian and in good standing, fully prepared for an eternal life in heaven. That did not mean I was ready to leave earth, not with two little boys and a wife I adore. The thought of leaving them was more torturous than any physical anguish I was experiencing.

I was thirty-three years old, and my life had never been filled with so many blessings and so much love. It's strange the things that run through your mind when death looms. I had the bizarre thought that I'd just finished a ten-year plan for my ministry, so God couldn't possibly want to take me now. Then I remembered the old saying, "Man plans and God laughs."

I also had the thought that God was piling on the Vujicic family. We were already grieving my father's dire diagnosis. And now I was feeling close to death myself.

Dad might outlive me, I thought. *This can't be the end.*

As they were preparing to prep me for surgery, I grew even more scared and panicked. I began crying and could not stop. My mum came to my side and asked what was wrong. I couldn't answer her through my pain and sobbing. I could hardly breathe.

My mother's faith is so strong. She leaned into me and whispered tenderly, "Don't you know if this is your time, it's okay, because you know where you are going? You will go to a much better place. So why are you so scared?"

All I could say in my head was, *I don't want to die; this can't be my time!*

FIGHTING FOR LIFE

I could tell from Mum's face and the serious expressions of the nurses that my life was in danger. This was not a drill. Nick might be going down. Someone said my blood pressure was still dropping. My catheter was clogged and created incredible pressure on my bladder. They were afraid to put me under with anesthesia because I was in such frail condition.

Suddenly my pain became so intense I arched my back and popped my entire body into the air, nearly launching myself from the hospital cart. They strapped me down and wheeled me out of the room.

"Stay with me, Mum," I begged. "Keep talking to me."

I was afraid I'd die on the way to the operating room. One minute I was looking up at the blinding fluorescent lights on the ceiling, and then everything faded to black. It was surreal, like a movie. Was my life fading to black? I was truly afraid to close my eyes, fearful that I'd die or go into a coma because of all the blood I'd lost.

She whispered, "Pray, Nick. Keep praying."

"Keep talking, Mum. Don't let me close my eyes!"

I wasn't being dramatic. The medical professionals were freaking out too. Later my mum told others in the family, "In that moment, I thought we might be losing Nick."

Finally, they were able to give me an anesthesia and sleeping gas. They couldn't give me that until I had an IV in. I slept in the hospital for two days. I'd lost a third of my blood volume. That's not good for anyone, but even a little blood loss is a problem for me, because the critical red blood cells are produced by our body's biggest bones in our legs and arms. I don't have those bones. My blood replacement abilities are much more limited than most.

Just when things settled down, I had another traumatic experience. The nurse and aides were preparing to take me into a restroom for a hot shower as they readied me to go home. They disconnected my IVs, and the nurse left my room to get towels. She'd been gone only a few seconds when it felt like my left lung collapsed. The sensation was like freezing water flowing into my lung. Then my right lung did the same thing. I called out to the nurse in a panic.

"I can't breathe! Get me oxygen," I croaked.

Within seconds the rapid-response team was swarming all over the room. It seemed like there were at least twenty of them. I thought I was going into shock, and then, suddenly, all the pain in my chest was gone and I felt fine. My doctor later said it was a vagal shock, which is a fainting spell brought on by low blood pressure or even getting up too quickly after lying down for a prolonged period.

That was much better news than I'd expected. In fact, I was released from the hospital later that day. I had to stay in bed for ten days after I got home. My energy level ranged from lethargic to zombie.

I had to cancel several speeches and preaching engagements. Mum came over to help out. She slept in my room the first few nights to keep an eye on me so Kanae could take care of the kids.

A CONVERSATION WITH GOD

The first night home I dreamed I was covered with blood on a battlefield, but it was not my blood. I had arms and legs and I was dressed like a marine. I was helping a friend pile sandbags in a trench. We were mired in mud. Guns were firing and bombs were exploding. Then a cloud descended to just a few feet off the ground, and between the cloud and me there arose a figure shimmering like a majestic gilded rose that filled the sky.

I knew this was God the Father. He spoke to me in this amazing, compelling voice: *I need you to come home. I need you up here. Please come.*

There was a tone of deep concern and urgency, like that of a parent calling home a child because of a family emergency: "You need to get home right now."

In the dream, I put my palms up and asked, "What do you mean?"

The voice of God again implored me, *I need you up here. Please come.*

This had to be a dream, because I then got a little bold with God the Father. I can't imagine doing that for real. I pointed to the raging battlefield around me and said, "You need me here, not there." Then I turned away and made a swatting motion, as if to say, "Don't bother me anymore. I have work to do."

Still dreaming, I went back into the trench, and within a couple of seconds there was the sound of a shot, and a bullet hit me in the back and came through my chest. Then I woke up with a startle and heavy breathing, and all I could think about was how wonderful it was to hear the voice of God, which was so beautiful, and the colors of the clouds. Then my mind and heart got anxious, wondering, *What does this dream mean?*

I don't know what that dream meant. I told my dad and my uncle Batta about it. One of them said, "You just told God you want to continue with your work on earth instead of going home to Him."

I don't know how much significance you should attach to dreams. This was very powerful, which is understandable, since I'd just gone through a traumatic, emotional experience. Maybe God was sending me a message. Perhaps He was telling me that He, too, believes in the importance of my mission to inspire others to believe in Him and follow Him.

Thank the Lord, the result on the biopsy they'd taken from my bladder was negative for cancer. Our prayers were answered, which meant we prayed all the more in thanks. My uncle Batta, who is always a source of wisdom, says that even a minor problem can become a major one if you don't get prayer around you. We definitely rallied the prayer chain for this challenge. I hope everyone continues to pray. I will probably need at least one more operation to correct the problems that still exist due to built-up scar tissue.

I thank God for allowing me to continue His work here. I ask for His help because I depend on Him just as we all do in this life.

STRENGTH THROUGH ADVERSITY

As a younger guy, I believed God would guide me through any challenge because I was intent on doing His work. I've learned in recent years that God also allows us to be challenged to test our faith. I feel like I've been through a few valleys and faced several fires personally and professionally in recent years. I certainly don't enjoy being tested, but I have to admit that I am stronger in faith than ever before.

The thought of growing strength through adversity came to mind recently after an experience with a hardworking guy hired to clean up some big trees that were hanging over the suburban Dallas house where Kanae's mother lives. One of the trees was dead and needed to come down entirely. The other was a beautiful tree, but it had some large limbs that posed a threat.

Esmeralda was worried they might damage her house if high winds and storms hit. When we visited her, I offered to help her find someone to remove the threatening limbs.

Friends recommended this guy; I'll call him Lorenzo. He was a short, wiry landscaper who drove a huge truck with a big trailer full of lawn mowers and tree-trimming equipment. We expected him to bring a crew of workers because these trees were very big. Instead, it was just Lorenzo.

I looked at the tree and then looked at him and wondered how he could possibly handle such a big job by himself. I thought he was just giving us an estimate. But after we agreed on his price, which was quite reasonable, he went to his truck and grabbed some ropes and a chainsaw.

I thought maybe he had the rope to secure himself to the tree for safety. Instead, he used it to tie the chainsaw to his waist. Then he began climbing the enormous dead tree like a human squirrel. He reached the upper portion of the tree, fired up the chainsaw to make it roar, and soon limbs were dropping from the sky.

Waaawaaa . . . crash!

Waaawaaa . . . crash!

Lorenzo obviously knew what he was doing, because in less than a half hour, there was nothing but a stump left of the dead tree. Surrounding it was a huge pile of logs and limbs. Lorenzo next went to work cutting up the logs and limbs and putting them in his trailer to haul off.

The sky darkened with menacing clouds, so I thought Lorenzo would pack up and come back another day to trim the other tree. When I looked out the window to check on him, I saw him look at the sky and then at the tree.

Before I could go outside, he put a ladder against the house and climbed up to the roof, his chainsaw again dangling from the rope around his waist. Without any wasted movements, he pulled the starter on the chainsaw and cut into one limb after the other, making sure they fell to the ground and not on the house.

Waaawaaa . . . waaawaaa.

Twenty minutes later he was on the ground, cutting up the pieces to add them to the pile in the trailer. When the wail of his chainsaw went silent, I went out to pay him.

"You are fearless, and you work very fast!" I said in Spanish. "I don't know how you did all that by yourself."

Lorenzo smiled as he wiped the sweat from his brow and neck with a handkerchief. "I asked my crew to work with me, but they said there was a storm coming. So I just decided to do it by myself," he said.

I told him we were impressed by how hard and how fast he worked, and he replied with the following story.

"When I was six years old, I began working on my parents' farm in my native country, and my responsibility was to look after the goats. I would go out in the pasture with them. There were no trees out there, so whenever a storm came, there was nowhere to hide. Sometimes there would be hail. Getting hit by the hail was the worst pain in my life. I would scream and get bruises all over my body, but I still had to keep the goats together and protect them. I learned to deal with the pain, and it made me strong. I am not afraid to work now under any conditions."

When God puts us through tests, and our prayers for His strength are answered, we emerge stronger in faith and in character. We come away more prepared for the challenges that will follow. Lorenzo climbed that tree with the confidence of a man who had weathered many storms since childhood. He is physically strong, yes, but even stronger in faith and character.

We all face storms. We have good months and bad months, good years and bad years. How we handle ourselves in the worst of times determines how we fare in the best of times.

I will never tell you that God wants you to be rich. I will never tell you that He wants you to have a comfortable life. I have read too much evidence in the Bible that says we need to prepare for the storms and the trials. We need to consider them with joy because the storms produce patience and faith.

The apostle Paul asked God three times to take a thorn from his flesh. What did God say? "My grace is sufficient for you, for my power is made perfect in weakness." In response, Paul wrote, "Therefore I will boast all the more gladly of my weaknesses, so that the power of Christ may rest upon me" (2 Corinthians 12:9).

As I understand this scripture, Paul was having visions and revelations that could have made him feel prideful or conceited, but the thorn in his side was a reminder to remain humble. Many Christians have theorized that Paul's thorn was actually a metaphor for an illness that God used to remind the apostle that good health is a blessing and we all need to pray for God's strength.

Don't feel victimized by ill health or hard times; instead, use those seasons to build upon your faith and to pray more than ever before. The additional benefit will be the wonderful example you provide for others to follow as a Christian whose faith only grows stronger when it is tested. God's grace is sufficient. His power is made perfect in our weakness.

My wish for you now as you complete your reading of this book is that you feel stronger as a Christian and that you will be inspired to draw upon your faith when faced with challenges in life. I also hope you are encouraged to share your faith with those who've yet to join your walk with the Lord Jesus Christ. In these pages, you've read many examples of ways you can do that. I hope some of them have inspired you to find your own so you, too, can one day walk through the gates of heaven surrounded by those you've recruited to join you in a joyful everlasting life.

SHARING THE GOSPEL

News Updates from Nick

The year 2017 has been a very special year for all of Europe with many celebrations of the five hundredth anniversary of the beginning of the Protestant Reformation. Because of this important historical observance, I was offered the opportunity to speak in countries like Italy, France, Switzerland, Belarus, and Ukraine, where I could appear on television or Internet livestreams to speak and share the gospel with millions of people.

As I wrote the final words for this book, I was feeling jet-lagged yet preparing to speak to four thousand students in Sochi, Russia. I had already spoken in Kiev, Ukraine. There, eight hundred thousand people gathered on Khreshchatyk, the main street downtown, while thousands of others watched on television. The message was translated into twenty languages across twenty-six other countries.

On the stage with me in Kiev was my dear friend Joseph Bondarenko. I consider him a part of my family. Joseph told the massive crowd why the Reformation was personally important to him. Decades earlier, he had been "most wanted" by the KGB because of his faith. They arrested him not far from this same stage and had him imprisoned. What closure this was for Joseph, my brother in Christ, who now proclaimed that Jesus is Lord and shared his testimony—close to the very spot where he was arrested.

At the end of my talk, I asked if anyone wanted to start their faith journey with Jesus as their Lord and Savior. We estimate that four hundred thousand people in Kiev raised their hands, indicating they were repenting of their sins and asking God to take over their lives. Beyond this unbelievable and exciting response, I wonder how many others watching on television also made this decision?

My wife, Kanae, and I began that day on the phone—both crying because there was no guarantee that terrorists would not try to disrupt the meeting. The stage was surrounded by tall buildings with many windows high above that left me exposed to potential shooters. We know there is always a chance we will be called home to heaven unexpectedly; on that day I definitely imagined some worst-case scenarios. But we walk forward one step at a time, and God always gives us courage and faith.

In Ukraine I was so honored to work with a group of organizers who put the event together with the approval of the government. These same organizers also helped me come to Ukraine in 2016 to meet with government officials and lead a prayer with all of them on their knees. That event also appeared on live television. Later we learned from the broadcasting company that out of the programming they'd done in the previous five years, this eighty-minute segment with the members of the national government was the most-watched program of all.

To be able to walk into countries where the government and national media open their arms and welcome me to share my story is truly a miracle. I love 1 Corinthians 1:27, which says, "God chose what is foolish in the world to shame the wise."

We know God can use us all, and we each have a story. I hope that my story instills faith and courage in you to see what God can do in you and through you, where you see that He truly is the God of the impossible.

THE ALBUM

I had seen Tyrone Wells in concert and had witnessed how his songs moved the spirit of those listening. He is a Christian, but his lyrics describe his faith and hope in Jesus without saying the J-word. Tyrone is now a good friend, and in 2010, our ministry took on a big undertaking and I recorded one of his songs, "More."

We made a music video for it and titled it "Something More," with the hope that many people would be touched and inspired. I was able to squeeze a mini-testimony into the video, and so far more than six million people have viewed it on YouTube. The positive comments have made the whole project worthwhile.

Because I know that God uses stories to inspire faith, our team gathered some friends—Jon Phelps, Tyrone Wells, Jordan Frye, and Kellen Mills—to write songs together. And now, my dream of releasing a debut album is a reality. Learning how songs are created has taken me to a whole new level of passion for music and appreciation for how God can "download" songs.

Then, coincidently, during a call with my book publisher, I was asked if I could write a song about "being the hands and feet." The publisher had no idea that I'd already started working on an album! I was so excited and responded with, "Absolutely!" So with Tyrone and Jordan, these are the lyrics we saw come to life:

Hands and Feet

He can take your broken pieces
He can make them beautiful
If you could only see what He sees

He can heal a heart that's hurting
He can find you in the dark
If you could only see what He sees

God take my hands and feet
You can have all of me
Come be my everything
Jesus

You are the Prince of Peace
You set the captive free

You are my everything
Jesus

In this place of desperation
Reaching out for something real
There's a love that changes everything

Let my life be a reflection
When the world looks at me
Jesus be the only one they see
To love the ones in need
The way that You love me

We hope to release the album, titled *Brighter World,* in 2018, and we pray that many are touched by the stories behind each song.

ACKNOWLEDGMENTS

I am grateful beyond words for my literary agent, Dupree Miller & Associates; my publisher, WaterBrook; and my ghostwriter, Wes Smith, for all believing in me and helping get my words out through books that have been translated into more than fifty-five languages.

I am so thankful for those who believed in my ministry early on when I started preaching as a teenager in Australia, and for those who helped make possible my move to the United States to establish Life Without Limbs (LWL) in Southern California—George Miksa and Elizabeth Gavrilovic, as founding employees, and my uncle Batta Vujicic as a founding board member. God also used David Price to fund the operations of LWL in its first year, and he therein became a board member. Thank you to the staff of LWL for all your support and hard work over the years of ups and downs.

I am in awe of how far we have come as a ministry. God brought us these crucial people: board members, advisory board members, incredible staff, the team coach from Aria, those who pray for us daily, those who consistently support us financially, the global coordinators, and so on.

I want to thank each person who has prayed for our ministry and believes in what God has called us to do. We are so thankful that God continues to place us on stages and paths to break down barriers and build bridges between people and the hope and love of Jesus Christ. We are grateful for all the churches that allow me to share my testimony in person and simulcast that message far and wide. We especially thank the churches in Southern California that have given us courageous and faith-filled support with our new tent outreaches.

I am also so pleased that we are producing libraries of videos and subtitling them in many different languages. And I am thankful for the prison ministry, as well as the evangelism accomplished with our friends at Teen Challenge. Thank you to One Voice Student Missions and their partnership in seeing more Bible clubs formed in public middle and high schools, as well as empowering churches to mobilize as missionaries to these campuses.

I am thankful for Attitude Is Altitude (AIA), which gets me into places I cannot yet openly preach the gospel. A great blessing to me and my family is my brother, Aaron, who helps navigate these motivational speaking opportunities worldwide, including training and coaching. We are also developing an education resource company and working to be involved in the film industry.

Everything I do is to plant seeds of hope, faith, and love. Whether through film and song, speaking to students about bullying, or government addresses about the integration of special-needs children into society, I do it with all my heart and with the focus that in all things, people may be drawn to the truth of their purpose-filled lives in God.

I look at my family and am so thankful for the love I've received in my life. However, there is no one who I am more thankful for than my soul mate, Kanae. Tears come to my eyes every time I am on the road, as I am in awe of who she is. At church with her not long ago, when the pastor was talking about temptation and the fruit of the Spirit, I told her that I truly married a holy woman. She laughed and said, "Oh, babe, I'm not holy." But I want you to know how blessed I am to have married a woman who is closest to holy. She is my rock and everything, and she pushes me closer to God. We love each other so much, and we know we have just begun this incredible journey together, along with two children . . . and two more by the time you read these words!

Kanae, I love you with all of my heart. You are and always will be my best friend and the greatest gift I could have ever imagined. I am so blessed to live life with you and see God move in and through our lives!